A Practical Guide for Policy Analysis

Sixth Edition

Sara Miller McCune founded SAGE Publishing in 1965 to support the dissemination of usable knowledge and educate a global community. SAGE publishes more than 1000 journals and over 800 new books each year, spanning a wide range of subject areas. Our growing selection of library products includes archives, data, case studies and video. SAGE remains majority owned by our founder and after her lifetime will become owned by a charitable trust that secures the company's continued independence.

Los Angeles | London | New Delhi | Singapore | Washington DC | Melbourne

A Practical Guide for Policy Analysis

The Eightfold Path to More Effective Problem Solving

Sixth Edition

Eugene Bardach

University of California, Berkeley

Eric M. Patashnik

Brown University

FOR INFORMATION:

CQ Press

An imprint of SAGE Publications, Inc.

2455 Teller Road

Thousand Oaks, California 91320

Email: order@sagepub.com

SAGE Publications Ltd.

1 Oliver's Yard

55 City Road

London EC1Y 1SP

United Kingdom

SAGE Publications India Pvt. Ltd.

B 1/I 1 Mohan Cooperative Industrial Area

Mathura Road, New Delhi 110 044

India

SAGE Publications Asia-Pacific Pte. Ltd.

18 Cross Street #10-10/11/12

China Square Central

Singapore 048423

Acquisitions Editor: Scott Greenan

Editorial Assistant: Lauren Younker

Production Editor: Bennie Clark Allen

Copy Editor: Melinda Masson

Typesetter: C&M Digitals (P) Ltd.

Proofreader: Sarah Duffy

Indexer: Jean Casalegno

Cover Designer: Anupama Krishnan

Marketing Manager: Jennifer Jones

Library of Congress Cataloging-in-Publication Data

Names: Bardach, Eugene, author. | Patashnik, Eric M., author.

Title: A practical guide for policy analysis : the eightfold path to more effective problem solving / Eugene Bardach, University of California, Berkeley, Eric M. Patashnik, Brown University.

Description: Sixth edition. | Washington, D.C. : CQ Press, [2020] | Includes bibliographical references and index.

Identifiers: LCCN 2018059104 | ISBN 9781506368887 (pbk. : alk. paper)

Subjects: LCSH: Policy sciences. | Decision making. | Problem solving.

Classification: LCC H97 .B37 2020 | DDC 320.6—dc23

LC record available at https://lccn.loc.gov/2018059104

SUSTAINABLE FORESTRY INITIATIVE
Certified Chain of Custody
At Least 10% Certified Forest Content
www.sfiprogram.org
SFI-01028

19 20 21 22 23 10 9 8 7 6 5 4 3 2 1

Contents

Preface

This handbook serves as a guide to concepts and methods applied in the analysis of policy. Eugene Bardach developed the general approach and many of the specific suggestions over thirty-five years of teaching policy analysis workshops to first- and second-year graduate students at the Richard and Rhoda Goldman School of Public Policy, University of California, Berkeley. In the handbook's earliest incarnation, the ideas took form slowly and were conveyed to students in lectures. But because Bardach and his faculty colleagues systematically overloaded their students with work, the students would sometimes skip a lecture—and thus miss out on ideas that he regarded as essential. Bardach determined that if he were to create a handout for the students, at least he would be discharging his responsibility, and it would be up to the students to retrieve the ideas they missed. Over the years, as the handout grew, it was disseminated informally to colleagues at other universities and was posted on the website of the Electronic Hallway, based at the University of Washington. This book is the outgrowth of these previous compilations and the product of many years of experience.

Eric M. Patashnik was first exposed to the Eightfold Path when he took the Introductory Policy Analysis course as a student at the Goldman School in the spring of 1988. As a professor, he has assigned earlier editions of Gene's book to hundreds of public policy students at UCLA, the University of Virginia, and Brown University.

The presumed user is a beginning practitioner preparing to undertake a policy analysis, such as one of our master's students at Berkeley or Brown. But we have found this handbook useful at both ends of the spectrum—in teaching undergraduate Introduction to Public Policy courses as well as executive education groups.

The handbook assumes a familiarity with basic economic concepts, including those having to do with market failures (including market imperfections). It is not meant to stand alone but should be used in conjunction with other sources, including some of the best textbooks in policy analysis, which are cited often to amplify points in this handbook: Behn and Vaupel (1982); Friedman (2002); MacRae and Whittington (1997); Morgan and Henrion (1990); Stokey and Zeckhauser (1978); and Weimer and Vining (2011). A book similar in spirit to this one, and that has many examples drawn from New Zealand and Australia, is Scott and Baehler (2010).

This new edition of *A Practical Guide for Policy Analysis* incorporates up-to-date examples of the concepts of policy analysis and features excerpts from real-world reports to illustrate each step of the Eightfold Path. It also contains a new appendix providing suggestions to analysts who wish to use "Big Data" and rigorous scientific evidence in their work, offers suggestions for projecting the "unintended" consequences of policy alternatives, and emphasizes the importance of thinking dynamically about adoption and implementation.

Finally, even with the addition of new material, or perhaps especially with these additions, we trust there is continuity with the spirit of previous editions. That spirit is about posing the right questions before moving on to search for the right answers. It is also about helping the reader/user under challenging intellectual, political, and logistical pressures to fend off confusion and anxiety. This is meant to be a friendly sort of book.

Acknowledgments

We wish to acknowledge the patience and helpful response of the students, friends, and family members who have provided helpful suggestions for improving this handbook, especially those who withstood its earlier versions. Special thanks are due Dan Acland, Nancy Bardach, Naomi Bardach, Rebecca Bardach, Mary Ann Bates, Robert Behn, Joy Bonaguro, Sandford Borins, Henry Brady, Jeanine Braithwaite, David Breneman, José Canela-Cacho, Eileen Chou, Ben Converse, Hank Dempsey, David Dery, John Ellwood, Lee Friedman, David Garcia-Junco Machado, Chloe Gibbs, Nina Goldman, Debbie Gordon, Justine Hastings, David Kirp, Jake Lavin, Leo Levenson, Martin A. Levin, Randall Lutter, Duncan MacRae, Christine Mahoney, Sarah Marxer, Carolyn Marzke, Jane Mauldon, Maria McKee, John Mendeloff, Michael O'Hare, Steven Page, Beryl Radin, Andres Roemer, Larry Rosenthal, Jesse Rothstein, Chris Ruhm, Mark Sabean, Jim Savage, Ray Scheppach, Peter Schuck, Elsa Schultze, Jay Shimshack, Bill Shobe, Eugene Smolensky, Alicia Sutton, Patrice Sutton, Craig Volden, David Weimer, Evan White, Jim Wyckoff, and Marc Zegans.

We wish to extend our thanks to our reviewers for their help with this edition: Kimberly Ratcliff, The Ohio State University; Ronald G. Shaiko, Dartmouth College; and Kimberly Speers, University of Victoria. Thanks also go to Scott Greenan, Lauren Younker, Bennie Clark Allen, Sarah Duffy, Jennifer Jones, and Melinda Masson for their help in bringing this new edition to press.

Sasha Dobrovolsky deserves our gratitude more than anyone else, however. Sasha was in Bardach's undergraduate Public Policy 101 class in 1991. An unusually gifted and entrepreneurial fellow, he once accosted his teacher with this announcement: "Professor Bardach, these handouts you give us are outstanding. You should publish a book. When I graduate, I'm creating my own publishing house, and your book is the first I'm putting out." Bardach said, "Sasha, you are surely mad. It's fine by me, but I am not going to be responsible for your financial losses. You are on your own." Sasha did exactly as promised. Alas, his publishing venture, Berkeley Academic Press, did not last long, but he went on to great success in other fields. We have unaccountably neglected to thank Sasha in the preface to some earlier editions. We hope we are now making sufficient amends.

Finally, we wish to thank our families for their love and support: Nancy, Naomi, Rebecca, and Elizabeth Bardach, and Debbie Gordon, Michael Patashnik, and Josh Patashnik.

SAGE and the authors would like to thank the following instructors for their invaluable feedback during the development of the fifth edition:

Jeanine Braithwaite, *University of Virginia*

Beth Greenberg, *Shippensburg University of Pennsylvania*

Mack Shelley, *Iowa State University*

Deborah Stine, *Carnegie Mellon University*

Jessica Ulm, *Indiana University–Bloomington*

About the Authors

Eugene Bardach has been teaching graduate-level policy analysis workshop classes since 1973 at the Goldman School of Public Policy, University of California, Berkeley, in which time he has coached some five hundred projects. He is a broadly based political scientist with wide-ranging teaching and research interests. His focus is primarily on policy implementation and public management, and most recently on problems of facilitating better interorganizational collaboration in service delivery (e.g., in human services, environmental enforcement, fire prevention, and habitat preservation). He also maintains an interest in problems of homeland defense, as well as regulatory program design and execution, particularly in areas of health, safety, consumer protection, and equal opportunity. Bardach has developed novel teaching methods and materials at Berkeley, has directed and taught in residentially based training programs for higher-level public managers, and has worked for the Office of Policy Analysis at the US Department of the Interior. He is the recipient of the 1998 Donald T. Campbell Award of the Policy Studies Association for creative contribution to the methodology of policy analysis, and is a fellow of the American Academy of Arts and Sciences. This book is based on his experience teaching students the principles of policy analysis and then helping them to execute their project work.

Eric M. Patashnik is the Julis-Rabinowitz Professor of Public Policy, a professor of political science, and the director of the master of public affairs program at the Watson Institute for International and Public Affairs, Brown University. He is also a nonresident senior fellow at the Brookings Institution and a fellow of the National Academy of Public Administration. Before coming to Brown, Patashnik held faculty positions at the University of Virginia (UVA), UCLA, and Yale University. During his time at UVA, he served as associate dean and acting dean at the Frank Batten School of Leadership and Public Policy. Patashnik's research focuses on the politics of American national policymaking, especially health policy, the welfare state, and the reform process. He is the author or editor of seven books. Patashnik has twice won the Louis Brownlow Book Award of the National Academy of Public Administration and has also won the Don K. Price Award of the American Political Science Association. Patashnik received his master of public policy and doctoral degrees from the University of California, Berkeley. Earlier in his career, Patashnik was a legislative analyst for the US House Administration Subcommittee on Elections.

Introduction

Policy analysis is a social and political activity. True, analysts take moral and intellectual responsibility for the quality of their policy-analytic work. But policy analysis goes beyond personal decision-making. First, the subject matter concerns the lives and well-being of large numbers of their fellow citizens. Second, the process and results of policy analysis usually involve other professionals and interested parties: it is often done in teams or office-wide settings; the immediate consumer is a "client" of some sort, such as a hierarchical superior; and the ultimate audience will include diverse subgroups of politically attuned supporters and opponents of the analysts' work. All of these facts condition the nature of policy analysis and have a bearing on the nature of what is meant by "quality work."

A policy analyst can work in any number of positions. Once upon a time, the term implied a rather wonkish individual who worked in a large government bureaucracy, serving up very technical projections of the possible impacts of one or more policy alternatives to some undersecretary of planning. No longer. Today's policy analysts help in program evaluation, program design, program management, public communications, planning, budgeting, and other functions. They work alone, in teams, and in loose networks that cut across organizations. They work in the public, nonprofit, and for-profit spheres, both in the United States and abroad. Although their work is ideally distinguished by transparency of method and interpretation, the analysts themselves may explicitly bring to their jobs the values and passions of advocacy groups as well as the technical expertise of "neutral" civil servants. The professional networks in which they work may contain—in most cases, do contain—colleagues drawn from law, engineering, accounting, and so on, and in those settings the policy-analytic point of view has to struggle for the right to counter—or, better yet, synthesize—the viewpoints of these other professionals. Although policy-analytic work products typically involve written reports, they may also include briefings, slide presentations, magazine articles, television interviews, and the use of social media. The recipients of these products may be broad and diffuse audiences as well as narrowly construed paying clients or employers.

The advice in this handbook is directed both to policy analysts in practice and to students and others who, for whatever reasons, are attempting to look at the world through the eyes of a practitioner.

THE EIGHTFOLD PATH

Policy analysis is more art than science. It draws on intuition as much as on method. Nevertheless, given the choice between advice that imposes too much structure on the problem-solving process and advice that offers too little, most beginning practitioners quite reasonably prefer too much. We have therefore developed the following approach, which we call the Eightfold Path:

- Define the Problem

- Assemble Some Evidence

- Construct the Alternatives

- Select the Criteria

- Project the Outcomes

- Confront the Trade-Offs

- Stop, Focus, Narrow, Deepen, Decide!

- Tell Your Story

These steps are not necessarily taken in precisely this order, nor are all of them necessarily significant in every problem. However, an effort to define the problem is usually the right starting place, and telling the story is almost inevitably the ending point. Constructing alternatives and selecting criteria for evaluating them must surely come toward the beginning of the process. Assembling some evidence is actually a step that recurs throughout the entire process, and it applies particularly to efforts to define the problem and to project the outcomes of the alternatives being considered.

The primary utility of this structured approach is that it reminds you of important tasks and choices that otherwise might slip your mind; its primary drawback is that, taken by itself, it can be mechanistic.

The Problem-Solving Process

The problem-solving process—being a process of trial and error—is iterative, so you usually must repeat each of these steps, sometimes more than once.

The spirit in which you take any one of these steps, especially in the earliest phases of your project, should be highly tentative. As you move through the problem-solving process, you will probably keep changing your problem definition, as well as your menu of alternatives, your set of evaluative criteria, and your sense of what evidence bears on the problem. With each successive iteration, you will become a bit more confident that you are on the right track, that you are focusing on the right question, and so on. This can be a frustrating process, but it can also be rewarding—if you learn to enjoy the challenges of search, discovery, and invention.

Some of the Guidelines Are Practical, but Most Are Conceptual. Most of the concepts used will seem obvious, but there are exceptions. First, technical terms are sometimes employed. Second, some commonsense terms may be used in a special way that strips them of certain connotations and perhaps imports others. For the most part, all these concepts will become intelligible through experience and practice.

The Concepts Come Embedded in Concrete Particulars. In real life, policy problems appear as a confusing welter of details: personalities, interest groups, rhetorical demands, budget figures, legal rules and interpretations, bureaucratic routines, citizen attitudes, and so on. Yet the concepts described in this handbook are formulated in the abstract. You therefore need to learn to "see" the analytic concepts in the concrete manifestations of everyday life.

Caution: Sometimes, Some Steps Are Already Determined. Suppose your client says, "We need an extra million dollars to run this program in the next budget year: find it." Does the Eightfold Path apply to this "analysis"? In a limited way. The client has already defined the problem and narrowed the relevant criteria very tightly. There won't be much creative scope for you when it comes to those steps. But all the other steps are likely to be relevant.

This challenge to "find it" is a simplified version of a more complex challenge—to "design it," as in to "figure out [that is, 'design'] a way to protect this subway system from terrorist attack." Here, too, the problem definition step has already been settled by the client, though the other steps are likely to get the creative juices flowing. Ideas for dealing with design problems in general are introduced in Part III, "Handling a Design Problem."

Your Final Product

So what will your final product look like? Here is a very rough sketch of a typical written policy-analytic report:

- In a coherent narrative style, you describe some problem that needs to be mitigated or solved.

- You lay out a few alternative courses of action that might be taken.

- To each course of action, you attach a set of projected outcomes that you think your client or audience would care about, suggesting the evidentiary grounds for your projections.

- If no alternative dominates all other alternatives with respect to all the evaluative criteria of interest, you indicate the nature and magnitude of the trade-offs implicit in different policy choices.

- Depending on the client's expectations, you may state your own recommendation as to which alternative should be chosen.

As a complement or even alternative to a traditional prose report, your final product might take the form of a policy brief or PowerPoint presentation. This type of product is becoming more and more common as a result of the increasing premium on delivering clear, crisp messages to busy decision-makers.

- Using a visually attractive format, you focus the audience's attention on the key problem you analyzed and/or your main recommendation.

- You present a small number of figures that capture your key takeaway message (see Appendix E on "Big Data" and visualization tools).

- Your policy brief or PowerPoint presentation should be self-contained and make sense to someone who has not read your full prose report.

The Spirit of the Eightfold Path

The spirit of the Eightfold Path is, we hope, economizing and uplifting. Analyzing public policy problems is a complex activity. It is easy to get lost, to waste a lot of time, to become demoralized. Other manuals and textbooks in policy analysis are primarily concerned that you get the analysis "right," in some sense. This one should help in that respect, too. But, in addition, we hope that this handbook will help you to get it done with reasonable efficiency—and with a minimum of anxious confusion.

Finally, just as policy analysis originates in politics, so it concludes in politics. Political life has two sides: channeling conflict and building community. Policy analysis serves both sides. It channels conflict by showing that some arguments, and their proponents, are in some sense superior to others and deserve to win out. But it helps to build community by marking off potential common ground as well. This common ground is defined by the rules and conventions of rational discourse—where opponents may employ analytical procedures to resolve disagreements, or where they may discover that at least some seemingly irreducible values conflicts can be recast as dry-as-dust technical disagreements over how much higher a probability Policy A has than Policy B for mitigating Problem P. In short, policy analysis contributes to better governance in a democratic society by focusing debate on the real-world consequences of collective decisions.

OVERVIEW OF THE BOOK

This book is a compilation of many component parts. The primary component is Part I, describing the Eightfold Path and recommending heuristics to help you negotiate it.

Part II focuses on one particular step in the Eightfold Path: assembling evidence. It first appeared thirty-five years ago as a journal article, but we have since modified it and tried to integrate it better into the overall book in terms of both style and content. We include it because its objective is, we think, unique among the many prescriptive works in the social sciences and in journalism about data gathering and interpretation: it is, above all, concerned with using the researcher's time and energy efficiently.

In the first several editions of this book, Part I incorporated suggestions for analyzing not only conventional, discrete problems of policy choice (in which the analytic task is to craft an intervention that will improve an otherwise well-functioning system), but also more ambitious "design" problems (in which the system itself is broken or missing). Because the two generic types of problems were both covered in a single part, it was easy for readers to miss the subtle distinctions between them. Accordingly, this edition includes a Part III that pulls out the material on design thinking. We show how the steps of the Eightfold Path can be "crosswalked" to design "systems of action" that will generate desired outcomes when multiple elements are interdependent and need to work together.

Part IV addresses a specialized topic in policy analysis not dealt with in other works: making use of ideas—and specimens of "smart practices"—that are to be found in other sites. Imitation and adaptation are standard routes to progress (albeit occasionally, to regress) in other areas of life, so why not in public policy?

Previous editions of this book included sections of a RAND Corporation study on the relative worth of mandatory minimum sentences for drug dealers to give readers an example of a real policy analysis (Caulkins et al. 1997). In this edition, we have decided instead to illustrate the concepts of policy analysis by providing excerpts (together with web links) from a variety of reports from think tanks, research organizations, and government agencies. We have chosen this new approach for several reasons. First, there is no one-size-fits-all model of a policy analysis report. Policy analysis reports come in different forms, and analysts should tailor their studies, and the communication of their studies, to the specific problem and audience at hand. Second, we seek to demonstrate the array of substantive issues on which policy analysis can be performed. Finally, we wish to draw readers' attention to the diversity of modeling tools and data sources that policy analysts today are using to define problems, project outcomes, and cope with uncertainty. While we regard all the excerpted studies as professional work products, we hasten to add that our inclusion of a portion of a particular study should not be taken as an endorsement of the study's methodology, findings, or recommendations. Instructors using this book might consider having their students read the full studies and identify their respective strengths and weaknesses as an assignment or a classroom discussion topic.

Appendix A, "Things Governments Do," is a condensed survey of eleven types of governmental instruments for intervening in society. This edition also offers Appendix B, "Understanding Public and Nonprofit Institutions: Asking the Right Questions"; a newly expanded Appendix C, "Strategic Advice on the Dynamics of Gathering Political Support"; Appendix D, "Tips for Working with Clients"; and a new Appendix E, "Suggestions for Incorporating 'Big Data' and Rigorous Scientific Evidence into Policy Analysis." Appendix E discusses the expanding use of large administrative data sets and increasing reliance on field experiments and other sophisticated methods for causal inference in policy labs and a growing number of government agencies. This appendix offers tips for policy analysts who wish to come up to speed on this important development.

We have tried to keep the style simple and the text short. But the topics covered are numerous and complicated. The result is that the book is in some respects very dense. Our students tell us that the book should be treated not just as a quick and pleasurable read, which of course it is, but as a reference volume to be experienced again and again for its delicious subtleties. No doubt they are right.

PART I

The Eightfold Path

The analytic work in problem solving generally proceeds in a certain direction, from defining the problem at the beginning all the way to making a decision and explaining it at the end. But remember, this is a process much given to reconsidering, reviewing, and changing your mind—in other words, retracing your steps on the path before starting out once more. Also, in some cases, the client or, perhaps, the political situation has already narrowed and focused the analytic task to such a degree that you need not even bother thinking through some of the steps. The exposition that follows lays out a generic process that must be adapted to particular contexts.

STEP ONE: DEFINE THE PROBLEM

Your first problem definition is a crucial step: it gives you both a reason for doing all the work necessary to complete the project and a sense of direction for your evidence-gathering activity. And in the last phases of the policy analysis, your final problem definition will probably help you structure how you *tell your story*.

It is easy to get the problem definition step wrong. Analytic looseness can creep in, creating a muddle. For example, at a congressional hearing about regulation of social media, lawmakers expressed the following concerns about Facebook:

- Facebook is too big and needs to be broken up.

- Facebook does not exercise sufficient care about sharing the data with outside organizations.

- Facebook collects too much data in the first place.

- Facebook is causing ideological polarization.

- Facebook is vulnerable to political exploitation and is not doing enough to curb hate speech and fake news.

- Facebook is promoting addictive message products to children.[1]

Might some of these concerns form the basis for a usable problem definition? Possibly, but all of them would require much greater precision. Many of the above-mentioned concerns point not to problems but rather to policy options. Still others are merely claims (which may or may not be accurate) about Facebook or social trends. The following suggestions can help improve problem definitions.

Think of Deficit and Excess

Semantic Tip It often—but not always—helps to think in terms of deficit and excess. For instance:

- "There are too many homeless people in the United States."

- "The demand for agricultural water is growing faster than our ability to supply it at an acceptable financial and environmental cost."

- "California's population of school-aged children is growing by 140,000 per year, and our ability to develop the physical facilities in which to educate them is not growing nearly as fast."

It often helps to include the word *too* in the definition—as in "too big," "too small," "growing too slowly," or "growing too fast." These last two phrases (about "growing") remind us that problems deserving our attention don't necessarily exist today but are (at least potentially) in prospect for the future, whether near or distant.

However, it does not help to think in terms of deficit and excess when your problem is an already well-structured decision choice—for example, "Dump the dredging spoils either in the Bay or somewhere out in the Pacific Ocean." Nor does it help if your challenge is to invent *any* way to accomplish some defined objective—for example, "Find some grant funds to close the anticipated gap between revenues and expenditures." These decision- and invention-type challenges are problems *for* the policy analyst but are not the substantive sort of problems we are addressing in this section.

Make the Definition Evaluative

The idea of a "problem" usually means that people think there is something wrong with the world, but *wrong* is a debatable term. Even if everyone accepts the same facts, not everyone will agree that the facts you (or others) have defined as a problem really do constitute a problem, for each person may apply a different evaluative framework to these facts. For example, some people believe that the fact of a growing foreign-born share of the US population is a problem; others believe it is not. Unfortunately, there are no obvious or accepted ways to resolve philosophical differences of this type.

A common philosophical as well as practical question is this: "What private troubles warrant definition as public problems and thereby legitimately raise claims for amelioration by public resources?" It is usually helpful to view the situation through the "market failure" lens (Friedman 2002; Weimer and Vining 2011, chap. 5).[2] In its simplest formulation, market failure occurs when the technical properties of a good or service have one of the following effects:

- Making it hard to collect payment from all the potential beneficiaries—for instance, the large number of people who profit, albeit indirectly, from advances in basic science

- Making it hard to collect from the beneficiaries of consumption the true economic cost of making use of the good or service—such as the fresh air that vehicle owners use as a sink for their auto emissions

- Making it hard for consumers (and sometimes suppliers) to know the true qualities of the good or service they are acquiring—for instance, many repair-type services, including those performed by physicians as well as those performed by auto mechanics

- Making the cost of producing the marginal unit lower than the average cost within the relevant range of demand—such as a magazine article distributed via the internet

It is impossible to overestimate the importance of this point. In most—though not all—situations in which no actual market failures can be identified, people's private troubles *cannot* typically be ameliorated by even the most well-intentioned governmental interventions. Even when some amelioration is possible, there are usually many adverse side effects. In some cases, it may nevertheless be worthwhile to pay the price of these side effects, but such calculations must be done carefully and scrupulously.

Besides market failures, the main situations in which private troubles can warrant definition as public problems are these:

- Breakdowns of systems such as family relationships that occur largely outside markets

- Low living standards that arise precisely because markets do function well and do not reward individuals very generously if they lack marketable talents or skills

- The existence of discrimination against women and racial and other minorities

The existence of market failure does not guarantee that governmental intervention will improve the situation. Government may be unwilling or unable to act primarily in the interest of its citizens. Policymakers may lack needed information or capacity, and politicians and civil servants may have interests and agendas of their own. The incentives that government faces from the political environment may not lead it to maximize efficiency or promote a just distribution. Just as real-world markets may fail to realize the competitive ideal, so government may fail to advance the social good. While the theory of "government failure" (Weimer and Vining 2011, chap. 8) is not as well developed as the theory of market failure, scholars have identified three main sources of government failure:

- Problems of direct democracy, such as a majority imposing very high costs on a minority

- Problems of representative democracy, such as the influence of organized groups, the underweighting of diffuse interests (e.g., consumers), and the excessive discounting of policy effects (e.g., the costs of public employee pensions) that occur after the current election cycle

- Problems of government production and supply, such as administrative inflexibilities due to civil service or procurement rules

As the scope of government grows, an important task for the policy analyst is to identify whether and to what extent current policy interventions are failing to achieve their goals at acceptable cost or are otherwise falling short. Policy analysts thus have a key role in diagnosing and remedying both market failures *and* government failures.

Using Issue Rhetoric. Usually, the raw material for the evaluative aspect of your initial problem definition comes from your client and derives from the ordinary language of debate and discussion in the client's political environment— language that we call generically "issue rhetoric." Such rhetoric may be narrowly confined to a seemingly technical problem or broadly located in a controversy of wide social interest. In either case, you have to get beyond the rhetoric to define a problem that is analytically manageable and that makes sense in light of the political and institutional means available for mitigating it.

Use the raw material of issue rhetoric with care. It often points to some condition of the world that people don't like or consider "bad" in some sense, such as "decaying infrastructure," "corporate welfare," or "wage stagnation." These evaluations do not necessarily need to be taken at face value. You will sometimes wish to explore the philosophical and empirical grounds on which you, your client, or others in your eventual audience should or should not consider the alleged condition "bad." Furthermore, issue rhetoric may point to some alleged—but not necessarily real—cause of a troubling condition, such as "a shortage of physicians," "globalization," or "income inequality."

Issue rhetoric often has a partisan or ideological flavor. Although most ordinary Americans do not possess a consistent ideology, issue rhetoric is created by the more passionate and often more articulate individuals whose views tend to be uniformly extreme in one direction. The great ideological divide in most developed democracies concerns the role of government assistance and regulation in solving problems relative to reliance on self, kin, and neighbors. Self-reliance is generally presumed to be the ideal, but this is a rebuttable presumption. "Liberal" issue rhetoric typically offers many rebuttals, usually involving distrust of "the market," but only some of these rebuttals are grounded in realistic understanding of how markets do and do not work. "Conservative" issue rhetoric sometimes offers thoughtful defenses of "the market" but can also fall silent when favored business interests seek protectionist legislation. Because government as an institution is the chief alternative to private and community problem solving, liberals and conservatives alike ideologize the question of just how competent and trustworthy it is. Selective perception abounds on both sides of this argument, especially in today's polarized environment.

Generalities originating in issue rhetoric only sometimes suffice to settle concrete issues of policy choice and policy design, although economic theories of market failures and imperfections can often tell us when not to rely on the market, and public choice theories of government failure can often tell us when not to rely on the government (Glazer and Rothenberg 2001; Weimer and Vining 2011). Policy analysis typically bridges all political ideologies by reliance on the normative standard of "maximizing welfare" and on social science theorizing and evidence about the comparative advantages of different institutions for different purposes. Thus you want not simply to echo the issue rhetoric in your problem definition, but to use it as raw material for a provisional problem definition that you hope will prove analytically useful.

Note also that some issue labels may signify more than one problem. Depending on the audience, for example, "teenage pregnancy" may connote any or all of the following conditions: sexual immorality, the blighting of young people's and their children's life chances, exploitation of taxpayers, and social disintegration. Usually you will want to determine a primary problem focus, to ensure that the analysis does not get out of hand. But if the problems aren't too complicated, you may feel willing to define more than one.

"Uncertainty" Is the Problem That Evaluation Addresses

If you are evaluating how well some policy or program has been working, what "problem" are you working on? How does evaluation fit into the Eightfold Path framework?

Like all policy analysis, your work here is answering questions about the future. True, you are looking at the past, but the intention is to use your conclusions to shape future action. Depending on your assessment of past performance, the typical future action could be to expand the program, cut the program back, kill the program altogether, start it up in some additional site, or modify it in some way. But what exactly is past performance, how does this performance measure against evaluative criteria, and what aspects of program design and implementation seem to have produced that outcome? It is this uncertainty that your evaluative work is addressing; therefore "too much uncertainty" is the problem.

Quantify If Possible

Your problem definition should, insofar as possible, include a quantitative feature. Assertions of deficit or excess should come with *magnitudes* attached. How big is "too big"? How small is "too small"? How about "too slowly" or "too fast"? With regard to homelessness, how many homeless people are there in the United States? Or in the case of agricultural water, how many acre-feet of water are used now, and how does that amount compare with the demand in some specified future year (given certain assumptions about water pricing)? Exactly what is "our ability to develop physical facilities for water storage," and how do we expect it to grow, or shrink, over time?

If necessary, gather information to help you calibrate the relevant magnitudes. (See the discussion under "Step Two: Assemble Some Evidence.")

In many or most cases, you will have to estimate—or, more likely, "guesstimate"—the magnitudes in question. Sometimes you should furnish a *range* as well as a *point* estimate of magnitudes—for example, "Our best guess of the number of homeless persons in families is 250,000, although the truth could lie between 100,000 and 400,000."

Even if you cannot come up with good numbers yourself, qualitatively defining a *metric* that might be used to quantify the problem helps you make your problem definition more behavioral and concrete. It is better to say, "Too many people with annual incomes over $60,000 are living in subsidized apartments," than simply, "Too many relatively well-off people are taking advantage of low-rent public housing." The $60,000 value provides desirable texture and information about a threshold number that will serve in the promised analysis.

Diagnose Conditions That Cause Problems

Some problematic conditions are not experienced as troublesome per se by citizens but are perceived by them, or by analysts working on their behalf, to be causes of trouble. It is sometimes useful to diagnose at least one alleged condition of this type and to define it as a problem to be mitigated or removed—as in "One of the problems in the air pollution area is that states have not been willing to force motorists to keep their engines tuned up and their exhaust systems in proper order."

Semantic Tip Note that this sort of problem definition is not merely descriptive but is also diagnostic. It implicitly asserts that some condition, which people may or may not find troubling on its own, is an important cause of some other condition that is indeed troubling. Problem definitions that pretend to such diagnostic power can be useful, but they can also be treacherous. Suppose, after all, that the causal diagnosis is mistaken or misleading—for example, that states' unwillingness to enforce engine maintenance routines is *not* in fact a very important cause of air pollution. Because the term *definition* in some contexts connotes legitimate arbitrariness ("I'll define *justice* to mean . . ."), the causal claims implicit in diagnostic problem definitions can easily escape needed scrutiny. (See "Step Five: Project the Outcomes" for further discussion.)

Risky Conditions: "The Odds"

"The odds are too high that this nuclear reactor will suffer an accident in the next twenty-five years that will emit excessive radiation." This sentence does indicate a problem, but it is not something tangible, like "Too many cases of asthma are being reported in this neighborhood." It refers to risk and is stated in probabilistic language dealing with "the odds."

Semantic Tip Referring to the odds is a useful way to talk about anything that is uncertain in your analysis (not just the problem definition) where the probabilities of outcomes can be approximately described or at least debated. It can also refer to the risk that an alternative will not work out as planned, or the likelihood that a key political actor will remain in office in order to oversee policy implementation. It is an especially useful locution when talking about risks that are particularly resistant to precise quantification—for example, "The odds are that the US nuclear modernization program is causing other countries to look more favorably on acquiring nuclear weaponry themselves."

The odds formulation can also be used for specifying criteria. For instance, one could say that one criterion is "Maximize the odds that members of the Freedom Caucus will hold a majority on the Ways and Means Committee following the next election," or "Minimize the odds that the health department's new computer system for verifying benefit eligibility will crash upon rollout."

Work on Hypothetical Problems—Up to a Point

Often "the problem" is implicit in a statement by the client (or some concerned group) that if only some alternative practice ("solution," in a sense) were in place, the world would be much better off. The analyst is charged with evaluating the merits of this supposition. For example, "If we'd had an up-to-date purchasing department, we would have anticipated this price increase and stocked up on X beforehand." Because Purchasing has allegedly been slack with regard to anticipated price movements, public money has been wasted. But there is a potential confusion lurking here: This is a useful problem definition only if the allegation is true. If it is not true, this problem does not exist. Should the analyst go off in search of a solution to a problem that does not really exist?

The simple solution is to conceive of "the problem" as "hypothetical" (or "possible") rather than actual. It is perfectly reasonable to study a hypothetical problem while not committing oneself to a belief in its reality just yet. Commitment is deferred until the study is completed or nearly completed.

The idea of a "hypothetical" problem implies a troublesome question: Of the billions of "hypothetical problems" in the world, how do we recognize, and characterize, this one? Primarily, it is implied by the statement of the supposed solution. The bundle of hypothetical problems implied by "lack of an up-to-date purchasing department" is not so very large, and it is even further focused by the particular example given by the client, being obliged to pay a price for X that is higher than would have been necessary. In the real world, certain policy areas seem to generate more of these hypothetical problems than others. The leading one concerns waste and inefficiency: "If we do things this way, the results will be more efficient." Or: "Currently, our procedures waste a lot of time going back and forth, checking and rechecking, whereas that would all be minimized were we to do Y." Hence, if someone alleges that the failure to do something is a problem, see if you can reframe "the problem" as "(possibly) too much waste." Note the waste does not have to be of money only—it could be time or opportunities to improve output in a cost-effective way.

Identify Latent Opportunities

A special kind of problem is an opportunity missed. Is it not rather small-minded to think of policy analysis as devoted merely to the amelioration of problems? Might policy analysis not rise above the tedious and uninspiring business of patching and fixing? Can we not aspire to a world in which we can identify opportunities to do creative—not to say wonderful—things? "If it ain't broke, don't fix it" is a confining idea, and certainly policy analysts, policymakers, and public managers ought not to allow the problem focus to restrict the search for plausible opportunities. Unfortunately, the working agenda of most policy professionals is set by complaints, threats, worries, and troubles—often leaving little time or energy to think about improvements that no one has identified as needful. Still, if latent opportunities are really lying around, it would be a pity to ignore them.

Where do we find opportunities for creative policy improvements that haven't first been identified by complaints, threats, and so on? Relatively little academic or technical theory is available to answer this question.[3] Box I-1 contains a list that is suggestive.

Avoid Common Pitfalls in Problem Definition

Problem definition is a step beset by at least three pitfalls.

Semantic Tip *Defining the solution into the "problem."* Your problem definition should not include an implicit solution introduced by semantic carelessness. Projected solutions must be evaluated empirically and not legitimated merely by definition. Therefore, keep the problem definition stripped down to a mere description, and leave it open where you will look for solutions.

- *Don't say:* "There is too little shelter for homeless families." Inadvertently implying that "more shelter" is the best solution may inhibit you from thinking about ways to prevent families from becoming homeless in the first place. *Try instead:* "Too many families are homeless."

- *Don't say:* "New schools are being built too slowly." Simply assuming that "more schools" is the solution may inhibit you from thinking about ways to use existing facilities more efficiently or even to try forms of "distance learning." *Try instead:* "There are too many schoolchildren relative to the currently available classroom space."

A tip-off that you're probably smuggling an implicit solution into the problem definition is to hear yourself saying, "Aha, but that's not the real problem; the real problem is . . ." While there are better and worse ways to conceptualize a problem—or to solve a problem—it stretches ordinary usage too much to say that one problem could be "more (or less) real" than another.

Accepting too Easily the Causal Claims Implicit in Diagnostic Problem Definitions. We suggested earlier that conditions that cause problems may also

Box I-1 Some Generic Opportunities for Social Improvement That Often Go Unnoticed

Designing the architecture of choice. By varying the ways in which choices are presented to people, it may be possible to overcome cognitive biases that lead to poor decision-making. For instance, flipping the preselected, default choice (the choice people automatically receive if they do not actively indicate a preference) from "opt out" to "opt in" can increase participation rates in organ donation programs and employee savings plans.

Social norms marketing. People often wish to follow social norms, but they can't do so if they are unaware of them. For example, many college students believe they drink less alcohol than the average—and increase their consumption to be more like their peers. When the true drinking rate is disseminated, peer pressure to binge is greatly reduced.

Internalizing the social effects of individual decisions. Many opportunities exist to improve social welfare by removing incentives for individuals to ignore the spillover costs of their decisions. For example, introducing congestion tolls would reduce traffic congestion by discouraging drivers from using roads during peak hours.

Operations research strategies. By means of sequencing, timing, prioritizing, matching, clustering, and other such rationalizing arrangements, it may be possible to use a fixed stock of resources to achieve higher productivity than is possible otherwise. For instance, provided that traffic flow conditions are within certain parameters, high-occupancy-vehicle (HOV) lanes can maximize vehicle throughput in a fixed section of roadway.

Cost-based pricing. Discrepancies between prices and real costs present an opportunity for enhancing social welfare by adjusting prices to better reflect reality. For instance, removing rent controls would bring prices more into line with real housing costs.

By-products of personal aspirations. It is possible to structure new incentives or create new opportunities for personal advantage or satisfaction that can indirectly result in social benefit. For example, public-sector employers can offer to share the benefits of cost-reducing innovations with the employees who conceive them and implement them.

Complementarity. Two or more activities can potentially be joined so that each may make the other more productive. For example, increased public works construction can combat unemployment.

Input substitution. The world abounds in opportunities to substitute less costly inputs in a current production process while achieving roughly equivalent results. For instance, municipalities can hire lower-paid civilians to perform police clerical tasks rather than use expensive uniformed officers.

Development. A sequence of activities or operations may be arranged to take advantage of a developmental process. For example, a welfare agency can assess clients for employability and vocational interest before, rather than after, sending them out to search for a job.

Exchange. Unrealized possibilities for exchange can increase social value. Policymakers typically design policies to simulate market-like arrangements—for example, conducting pollution permit auctions, or reimbursing an agency for services it renders to another agency's clients or customers.

Multiple functions. A system can be designed so that one feature has the potential to perform two or more functions. For example, a tax administrator can dramatize an enforcement case in such a way as both to deter potential violators and to reassure nonviolators that they are not being played for suckers because of their honesty.

Nontraditional participants. Line-level employees of public agencies—as well as their customers, their clients, or the parties whom they regulate—often have knowledge of potential program improvements that could usefully be incorporated into the agencies' policies and operations. The Internal Revenue Service (IRS), for instance, has sought feedback from ordinary tax filers about how to improve federal tax forms.

Underutilized capacity. Governments sometimes systematically under-utilize resources at their disposal. In many communities, school facilities are used for relatively limited purposes for only part of the day and for only part of the year—although school officials would be quick to warn that tapping this capacity without harming school functions is not always easy.

be problems themselves. However, the causes must be real, not merely assumed. You have to evaluate the causal chain that goes from the situation itself to the bad effects it is alleged to cause, and to convince yourself that the causal relationship is real. For instance, for some people, cocaine use is not a problem in itself, but it may become a problem if it *leads to* crime, poor health, family disintegration, and so on. But does it lead to these outcomes, and to what degree? The evidence on this question should be evaluated very carefully before you decide that it's okay to work with a problem definition that sounds like "too much cocaine use." (See Appendix E on the use of experimental methods in policy analysis.)

It is easy to get causal attributions wrong and then follow a suboptimal path of searching and reasoning. Consider the problem of low vaccination rates. In some parts of the country, a significant fraction of parents delay or refuse to vaccinate their children out of a fear that vaccination causes autism. When local vaccination rates fall below 90–95 percent, communities lack "herd immunity," leaving children at risk of contracting vaccine-preventable diseases like measles. Given this, it is tempting to work with a problem definition like "too many parents believe vaccines cause autism" and focus on options to reduce vaccination misperceptions, such as public health information campaigns to educate people about the true benefits and harms of immunizing their children. But the presumed causal chain that goes from parental beliefs to vaccination rates may be wrong. And in fact studies have shown that pro-vaccination messaging may not be effective and can even backfire.[4] Further, research has shown that imposing strict school vaccination rules (which make it harder for parents to enroll children who haven't received required immunizations) significantly boosts vaccination rates.[5] In other words, changing people's minds about vaccinations may not be required to change their behavior.

Ignoring the Context of the Problem. Context makes a difference. Possible solutions that work in one place fail in another, and vice versa. This is not just because many public policy problems are very difficult, and often overwhelming, but because some contexts are favorable to a particular strategy while others are not. If context is likely to matter—and, even though it mostly does, that is not always the case—and problem contexts differ, problem definition should recognize this by specifying the contextual conditions under which the problem is likely to be encountered. For example, if public trust and confidence in the police is significantly influenced by neighborhood crime rates, the problem of "too little satisfaction with the police" should be defined at the local rather than national level.

Iterate

Defining the problem is a crucial step. (See Box I-2 for an illustrative specimen of a problem definition from a policy analysis report.) Because problem

Box I-2 An Illustrative Example of "Defining the Problem" from a Policy Analysis Report

From: Sheena McConnell, Irma Perez-Johnson, and Jillian Berk, "Providing Disadvantaged Workers with Skills to Succeed in the Labor Market," in *Policies to Address Poverty in America*, The Hamilton Project, June 2014, 98, http://www.hamiltonproject.org/assets/files/policies_address_poverty_in_america_full_book.pdf

The supply of skilled workers is not keeping up with the demand for them (Goldin and Katz 2012). Employers report shortages of workers with occupation-specific skills (Holzer et al. 2011). A recent survey of 2,000 U.S. companies found that 30 percent had been unable to fill skilled job positions for more than six months (Manyika et al. 2012).

Many low-income workers would not be able to access vocational training without assistance from government programs. Although the vast majority of vocational training in the United States is provided by employers (Mikelson and Nightingale 2004), employers are less likely to provide training for their lower-skilled positions, which tend to have higher rates of turnover (Lane 2000). Hypothetically, workers could pay for their own training, but many unemployed and low-skill workers do not have the financial resources or the ability to borrow to pay for training.

The United States does not currently invest heavily in vocational training compared with other countries, and funding for vocational training has declined over the past decades. Whereas the United States spends less than 0.05 percent of its gross domestic product on vocational training, other industrialized nations invest up to ten times as much. Since 1985 the amount budgeted for key U.S. Department of Labor training programs has declined by about 20 percent in real terms.

Even among supporters of vocational training, there is legitimate concern that many people who start programs do not complete them. Within three years of enrollment in a community college, fewer than half of all enrollees have attained an associate's degree or vocational certificate, transferred to a four-year institution, or remain in college (Horn and Weko 2009). Only about 55 percent of the people who begin two-year colleges obtain either an associate's degree or a certificate (Holzer and Dunlap 2013). Analysis of data on training vouchers provided by the WIA Adult and Dislocated Worker programs found that only 64 percent of workers who enrolled in training programs at community colleges completed a

(Continued)

(Continued)

training program within three years (Perez-Johnson, Moore, and Santillano 2011). Although the rate of completion for those enrolled in training at a private training provider was higher, about 15 percent of trainees still did not complete a training program within three years.

A second concern is that too many workers who complete training cannot subsequently find a job to use the acquired skills. A study of training vouchers provided through the WIA Adult and Dislocated Worker programs reported that only about 40 percent of the participants found employment in the occupation for which they received training (Perez-Johnson, Moore, and Santillano 2011). Similarly, a study of the Trade Adjustment Assistance program found that only 37 percent of people who participated in training funded by that program held a job in the occupation for which they were trained in the fourth year after they were initially laid off (Schochet et al. 2012). These statistics suggest that there is often a missing link between employers and training programs.

[Endnotes and references to figures omitted from excerpt.]

Source: Sheena McConnell, Irma Perez-Johnson, and Jillian Berk, "Providing Disadvantaged Workers with Skills to Succeed in the Labor Market," in *Policies to Address Poverty in America*, The Hamilton Project, 2014, p. 98.

definition is hard to get right, however, you may take that same step again and again. Also, your empirical and conceptual understanding will evolve over the course of your analytic work. For instance, you may start out thinking that the main problem is "too many halfway houses for the mentally ill in our city" but end up concluding that the main problem is how badly some of them are managed.[6] As you begin to rule out alternative approaches to solving or mitigating your problem, you will probably want to sculpt the problem definition so that, in the end, you and the political system will have some chance of attacking the problem successfully. Finally, if you are working in an office or agency context, you will implicitly be negotiating a mutually acceptable problem definition with your analyst colleagues and your hierarchical superiors.[7]

STEP TWO: ASSEMBLE SOME EVIDENCE

All of your time doing a policy analysis is spent on two activities: thinking (sometimes aloud and sometimes with others) and hustling data that can be turned into evidence. Of these two activities, thinking is generally the more important, but hustling data takes much more time: reading documents, hunting in libraries, poring over studies and statistics, interviewing people, traveling to interviews, waiting for appointments, and so on.

The real-world settings in which policy analysis is done rarely afford the time for a research effort that would please a careful academic researcher. In fact, time pressure is probably almost as dangerous an enemy of high-quality policy analysis as is politically motivated bias, if not more so. Therefore, economize on your data collection activities. The key to economizing is this: try to collect only those data that can be turned into "information" that, in turn, can be converted into "evidence" that has some bearing on your problem.

Semantic Tip For the logically minded, here are some definitions: *Data* are facts—or, some might say, representations of facts—about the world. Data include all sorts of statistics but go well beyond statistics, too. Data also include, for instance, facts about an agency manager's ability to deal constructively with the press. *Information* consists of data that have "meaning," in the sense that they can help you sort the world into different logical or empirical categories. The prevalence of cigarette smoking in five different countries constitutes data, but these data become information when you decide it is interesting to array the countries comparatively (e.g., from lowest to highest prevalence). *Evidence* is information that affects the existing beliefs of important people (including yourself) about significant features of the problem you are studying and how it might be solved or mitigated. Differential prevalence of smoking, for instance, can become evidence bearing on hypotheses concerning different levels of concern about personal health across countries.

You need evidence for three principal purposes, all of which are relevant to the goal of producing realistic projections of possible policy outcomes. One purpose is to assess the nature and extent of the problem(s) you are trying to define. A second is to assess the particular features of the concrete policy situation you are engaged in studying. For instance, you may need to know—or guess—about agency workloads, recent budget figures, demographic changes in a service area, the political ideology of the agency chief, the competency of the middle-level managers in the agency, and the current attitudes of some other agency that nominally cooperates with yours on some problem. The third purpose is to assess policies that have been thought, by at least some people, to have worked effectively in situations apparently similar to your own, in other jurisdictions, perhaps, or at other times. (Sometimes these situations will have been evaluated statistically and sometimes not: see Part IV, "'Smart (Best) Practices' Research: Understanding and Making Use of What Look Like Good Ideas from Somewhere Else.")

Because each of these purposes becomes salient in different phases of the policy analysis process, the second step on the Eightfold Path, "Assemble Some Evidence," will be taken more than once but with a different focus each time.

Think before You Collect

Thinking and collecting data are complementary activities: You can be a much more efficient collector of data if you think, and keep on thinking, about what you do and don't need (or want) to know, and why. The principal—and exceedingly common—mistake made by beginners and veterans alike is to spend time collecting data that have little or no potential to be developed into evidence concerning anything you actually care about. People often do this because running around collecting data looks and feels productive, whereas first-rate thinking is hard and frustrating. Also, when they see you busily collecting data, the people paying for your work tend to be reassured that somehow they are getting their money's worth.

The Value of Evidence. Since most evidence is costly to produce, you must weigh its likely cost against its likely value. How is its likely value to be estimated? The answer may be cast in a decision-analytic framework (decision trees), though remember that the process of making a decision involves a great many elements prior to the moment of actual choice, such as defining a useful problem, thinking up better candidate solutions, and selecting a useful model. In general, the value of any piece of evidence depends on these factors:

- The likelihood that it will cause you to substitute some better decision for whatever decision you would have made without it (which might have been an "acceptable" decision in and of itself)

- The likelihood that the substituted decision will, directly or indirectly, produce a better policy outcome than the outcome that would have been produced by the original decision

- The magnitude of the difference in value between the likely-to-be-improved outcome and the original outcome

The Utility of Research. Although evidence is costly to produce, there are instances when a high price may be worth paying. If the evidence required to understand a situation does not exist but could be assembled, analysts may choose to invest in substantial data generation efforts, which may range from qualitative interviews and case studies to quantitative modeling. (Box I-3 provides an example of modeling using a hard-edged engineering approach to estimate the greenhouse gas emissions from global oils. The evidence produced by the model is intended to serve as an input into the design of climate mitigation strategies for the "unconventional" energy resources being unleashed through technologies such as fracking.)

Box I-3 An Illustrative Example of "Assembling Some Evidence" from a Policy Analysis Report

From: Deborah Gordon et al., *Know Your Oil: Creating a Global Oil-Climate Index* (Policy Brief), Carnegie Endowment for International Peace, 2015, 3–4, https://carnegieendowment.org/files/know_your_oil.pdf

The character of oil is changing. Consumers may not notice the transformation—prices have fluctuated, but little else appears to have changed at the gas pump. Behind the scenes, though, the definition of oil is shifting in substantial ways. There is oil trapped tightly in shale rock, and oil pooled many miles below the oceans. Oil can be found in boreal forests, Arctic permafrost, and isolated geologic formations. Some oils are as thick as molasses or as gummy as tar, while others are solid or contain vastly more water or gas than normal.

Oil resources were once fairly homogeneous, produced using conventional means and refined into a limited number of end products by relatively simple methods. This is no longer the case. Advancements in technology mean that a wider array of hydrocarbon deposits in once-unreachable areas are now viable, extractable resources. And the techniques to turn these unconventional oils into petroleum products are becoming increasingly complex.

As oil is changing, so, too, is the global climate. The year 2014 ranked as the earth's warmest since 1880. Fossil fuels—oil along with coal and methane gas—are the major culprits.

The only way to determine the climate impacts of these previously untapped resources—and to compare how they stack up against one another—is to assess their greenhouse gas (GHG) emissions at each stage in the oil supply chain: exploration, extraction, processing, refining, transport, and end use. The more energy it takes to carry out these processes, the greater the impact on the climate. And in the extreme case of some of these oils, it may take nearly as much energy to produce, refine, and transport them as they provide to consumers. Moreover, each oil yields a different slate of petroleum products with different combustion characteristics and climate footprints.

The Oil-Climate Index (OCI) is a metric that takes into account the total life-cycle GHG emissions of individual oils—from upstream extraction to midstream refining to downstream end use. It offers a powerful, yet user-friendly, tool that allows investors, policymakers, industry, the public, and other stakeholders to compare crudes and assess their climate

(Continued)

(Continued)

consequences both before development decisions are made as well as once operations are in progress. The Oil-Climate Index will also inform oil and climate policy making.

The index highlights two central facts: The fate of the entire oil barrel is critical to understanding and designing policies that reduce a crude oil's climate impacts. And oils' different climate impacts are not currently identified or priced into the market value of competing crudes or their petroleum products. As such, different oils may in fact entail very different carbon risks for resource owners or developers.

Analysis of the first 30 test oils to be modeled with the index reveals that emission differences between oils are far greater than currently acknowledged. Wide emission ranges exist whether values are calculated per barrel of crude, per megajoule of products, or per dollar value of products, and it is expected that these emission ranges could grow as new, unconventional oils are identified.

There are several critical variables that lead to these variations in oils' life-cycle climate emissions. They include how gas trapped with the oil is handled by producers, whether significant steam is required for oil production, if a lot of water is present as the oil reservoir depletes, how heavy (viscous) or deep the oil is, what type of refinery is used, and whether bottom-of-the-barrel products like petroleum coke (known as petcoke) are combusted. Given these factors, the most climate-intensive oils currently identified—gassy oils, heavy oils, watery and depleted oils, and extreme oils—require special attention from investors, operators, and policymakers.

[See another excerpt from this report on coping with uncertainty in Step Five.]

Source: Deborah Gordon, Adam Brandt, Joule Bergerson and Jonathan Koomey, *Know Your Oil: Creating a Global Oil-Climate Index*, Policy Brief, Carnegie Endowment for International Peace, Washington, D.C., 2015, pp. 3–4.

The Utility of an Educated Guess.

It is surprising how well you can do in many cases by gathering no evidence at all but simply sitting down and thinking something through and then making some serious educated guesses. There is nothing shameful about acting on such guesstimates and thereby conserving your data-collecting time and energies for answering questions for which good evidence is really necessary (see Part II, "Assembling Evidence").

A helpful check on your thinking, to avoid collecting useless data, is to ask yourself the following questions before embarking on some data collection venture:

- "Suppose the data turn out to look like so-and-so as opposed to thus-and-such. What implication would that have for my understanding of how to solve this problem?"

- "Compared to my best guess about how the data will look once I've got them, how different might they look if I actually took the trouble to get them?"

- "How much is it worth to me to confirm the actual difference between what I can guess and what I can learn about the world by really getting the data?"

It is this sort of critical attitude about the value of expensive data collection (especially ad hoc surveys and "needs assessments"!) that often leads good and experienced policy analysts to make do with back-of-the-envelope estimates. However, none of this reasoning is meant to be an excuse for shirking the job of getting good data—and sometimes a lot of data, at huge costs in time and money—when you've convinced yourself that the investment really will pay off. There's an obvious and critical difference between justifiable and unjustifiable guesstimates.

Review the Available Literature

There hardly exists a problem on whose causes and solutions some academic discipline or professional association is not doing research. It is easy to find journals and various professional publications disseminating empirical results, theories, case studies, and so on. The internet brings much of this literature to your desktop. Studies vary in their quality, rigor, and internal and external validity. Policy analysts should evaluate research with a critical eye, focusing not only on a study's "bottom line" but also on the strengths and limitations of its research design and, especially, on the relevance of its findings to the problem-solving tasks at hand.[8]

Advocacy organizations often publish a great deal of interesting work and may take special pains to disseminate their findings on the internet. However, because advocacy-based analyses are not, in general, as reliable as more disinterested work, there is a danger of relying too much on such sources just because they are readily available.

Survey "Best Practices"

The chances are good that the problem you are studying is not unique and that policymakers and public managers in other jurisdictions, perhaps not very different from the one you are studying, have already dealt with it in some fashion. See if you can track down some of these past solutions and extrapolate them to the situation you are studying. Bear in mind, however, that the extrapolation process is complicated (see Part IV, "'Smart (Best) Practices' Research").

Use Analogies

Sometimes it pays to gather data about things that, on the surface, seem quite unlike the problem you are studying but, on a deeper level, show instructive similarities. For instance, your understanding of how a merit pay plan for compensating managers in the public sector might work could perhaps be improved by seeing how similar schemes work in the private sector. Or, if you are working on the problem of how a state can discipline, and perhaps disbar, incompetent attorneys, you might usefully spend a good deal of your time learning about how the medical profession handles problems of physician incompetence. If you are working on how to reduce neighborhoods' resistance to accepting low-income housing projects, you could usefully look into the literature on community resistance to accepting solid-waste incinerators.

As these examples suggest, some analogies are easier to perceive, and to make sense of, than others. It takes a little imagination to see an instructive analogy and, occasionally, is a little daring to try to convince others to recognize both its usefulness and its inevitable limitations.

Start Early

You are often dependent on the very busy schedules of other people whom you ask to furnish information or to make time for an interview. It is extremely important to submit requests for information—and especially for interviews— well in advance of when you want to have completed the data collection. (For a useful description of how to conduct literature reviews, library searches, phone interviews, and personal interviews, see Weimer and Vining 2011, chap. 14; see also Part II, "Assembling Evidence.")

Touch Base, Gain Credibility, Broker Consensus

The process of assembling evidence inevitably has a political as well as a purely analytic purpose. Sometimes it entails touching base with potential critics of your work so that they will not be able to complain later that you have ignored their perspectives. Conversely, by making yourself known to potential supporters of your work, you may be able to create a cadre of defenders.

A more complex objective, where appropriate, might be to blend policy analysis with the process of improving a policy idea or decision during the course of implementation. (See the following discussion of "improvability" as a practical criterion.) This objective entails obtaining feedback from participants, usually in an iterative process, and sharing some of your own reactions with them. You thereby become more of a partner in the process than an outside observer and diagnostician. An even more complex and challenging role would be for you to become a particular type of "partner," a facilitator and broker, whether by acting as a conduit from one person to another or by convening meetings and other gatherings.

Free the Captive Mind

In exchange for access to data and a ready-made worldview, researchers sometimes uncritically accept problem definitions and preferred solutions from kindly informants (not to mention from paying clients or employers). To counter such temptations, be sure to make contact with individuals or factions whom you would expect to disagree—the more sharply the better—with those informants. A time-saving, but only partial, substitute is to ask your kindly informants, "Who might object strongly to your point of view about this, and why might they do so?"

STEP THREE: CONSTRUCT THE ALTERNATIVES

By *alternatives*, we mean something like "policy options," or "alternative courses of action," or "alternative strategies of intervention to solve or mitigate the problem."

For example, the Congressional Budget Office (CBO) in 2013 analyzed four alternatives to the US Army's plan to develop a new Ground Combat Vehicle (GCV) as a replacement for the Bradley Infantry Fighting Vehicle (IFV): (1) purchase the Israeli Namer armored personnel carrier, (2) upgrade the Bradley IFV, (3) purchase the German Puma IFV, and (4) retain the current Bradley IFV.[9] See Box I-4 for an illustrative example.

Beware a Linguistic Pitfall

Semantic Tip   Specifying alternatives does not necessarily signify that the policy options are mutually exclusive. Policy analysts use the term *alternative* ambiguously: sometimes it means one choice that implies forgoing another, and sometimes it means simply one more policy action that might help to solve or mitigate a problem, perhaps in conjunction with other alternatives. Be aware of the ambiguity in other people's usage, and in telling your story (see Step Eight), be sure that no such ambiguity enters your own usage.

If it is impossible to implement two or more options separately—such as an increase in the length of the school day and a restructuring of after-school programs—it usually makes sense to combine them into a single policy option. Sometimes, though, you won't be entirely sure whether two alternatives are or are not mutually exclusive. For instance, although the mayor may have promised enough money to either fix potholes or provide homeless shelters (but not both), you may have made such a great case for both programs that the mayor may decide to increase the budgetary allocation. See the subsection under "Step Six: Confront the Trade-Offs" that advises you to rank your list of preferred alternatives so that it is up to the decision-maker to decide when enough is enough.

Start Comprehensive, End Up Focused

In the last stages of your analysis, you won't want to be assessing more than two or three principal alternatives, but in the beginning, err on the side of comprehensiveness. Make a list of all the alternatives you might wish to consider in the course of your analysis. Later on, you will discard some obvious losers, combine others, and reorganize still others into a single "basic" alternative with one or more subsidiary "variants." For your initial list, though, where should you turn for ideas?

One starting point would be to note the alternatives that key political actors are actively proposing or seem to have on their minds. These may include prominent people's pet ideas, institutions' inventories of "off-the-shelf" proposals that simply await a window of opportunity, and prepackaged proposals that party leaders or political ideologues are perennially advocating. Then you could try to *design* alternatives that might prove to be superior to the alternatives currently being discussed by the key political actors.

Entertain out-of-the-Box Solutions. It's good to brainstorm, to try to be creative. You might not produce much better ideas than those that other people have already advanced. But, then again, you might.

One way to coax your creativity is to refer to the checklist in Appendix A, "Things Governments Do." For each entry on the list, ask yourself: "Might it make sense to try some version of this generic strategy to help mitigate this problem?" Because it is a comprehensive list, the answer with respect to any single strategy will usually be no. Going through the list systematically is worthwhile, however. Because the list is not very long, with experience, you will need to spend only a few minutes to decide whether any ideas there might be worth considering further. (See also the valuable discussion about generic policy instruments in Weimer and Vining 2011, chap. 10.)

Another approach is to free your mind to consider unconventional, out-of-the-box solutions. To be sure, most of these ideas won't turn out to be workable for one reason or another; yet many good policy ideas used today (e.g., emissions trading programs) were considered odd or impractical when they were first proposed. Also, technological breakthroughs and changing social norms are continuously expanding the set of feasible solutions.

Following are some suggestions for coming up with a better mousetrap[10]:

- *Ask how you would solve a problem if cost were no object.* Of course, in the real world, cost *is* an object. But imagining it isn't can sometimes free the imagination. For example, if cost were no object, you would never wait in line at the post office—you would have an assistant mail your packages. But why couldn't there be a public website where citizens could find out the wait times at every post office—indeed, at every government agency that serves customers?

- *Ask where else it would work.* If a solution works in one context, maybe it would work in another. For example, a mathematical algorithm is used to match medical students with residency programs, minimizing the frequency of "bad" matches. Why shouldn't an algorithm also be used to match foster children or adoptive children with qualified adults who wish to be foster or adoptive parents?

- *Ask why not.* Many people are upset about the high cost of auto insurance. One reason people are right to complain is that insurance rates hardly vary with mileage. A flat-fee policy also discriminates against the poor, who tend to drive less. But why *shouldn't* insurance rates be charged on a per-mile basis? That would be fairer and more efficient. GPS devices could monitor the number of miles driven. To be sure, there are privacy concerns and other obstacles to overcome. But asking, "Why not?" often leads to creative thinking.

Semantic Tip Always include in your first approach to the problem the alternative "Let present trends (or 'business as usual') continue undisturbed." You need to do this because the world is full of naturally occurring, ongoing changes, some of which may mitigate, or worsen, the problem on which you are working. (Note that we are not characterizing this alternative as "Do nothing." It is not possible to do nothing or to "not decide." Most of the trends in motion will probably persist and alter the problem, whether for better or for worse.)

To see if "natural" change will affect the scope of the problem, inspect its most common sources in the public policy environment: (1) political changes following elections, as well as changes induced by the prospect of having to contest an election; (2) changes in unemployment and inflation rates that accompany the business cycle; (3) the changing "tightness" or "looseness" of agency budgets caused by overall taxing and spending policies as well as by program features such as automatic cost-of-living increases; (4) demographic changes, such as population migration patterns and population "bulges" moving through certain age levels; and (5) changing technologies. In most cases, however, this "let-present-trends-continue" option will drop out of your final analysis. It follows that if

Box I-4 An Illustrative Example of "Constructing the Alternatives" from a Policy Analysis Report

From: *Options to Manage FHA's Exposure to Risk from Guaranteeing Single-Family Mortgages*, **Congressional Budget Office, September 2017, 1-2, https://www.cbo.gov/publication/53084**

Summary

The Federal Housing Administration (FHA) insures the mortgages of people who might otherwise have trouble getting a loan, particularly first-time homebuyers and low-income borrowers seeking to purchase or refinance a home. During and just after the 2007–2009 recession, the share of mortgages insured by FHA grew rapidly as private lenders became more reluctant to provide home loans without an FHA guarantee of repayment. FHA's expanded role in the mortgage insurance market ensured that borrowers could continue to have access to credit. However, like most other mortgage insurers, FHA experienced a spike in delinquencies and defaults by borrowers.

Recently, mortgage borrowers with good credit scores, large down payments, or low ratios of debt to income have started to see more options in the private market. The Congressional Budget Office [CBO] estimates that the share of FHA-insured mortgages going to such borrowers is likely to keep shrinking as credit standards in the private market continue to ease. That change would leave FHA with a riskier pool of borrowers, creating risk-management challenges similar to the ones that contributed to the agency's high levels of insurance claims and losses during the recession.

This report analyzes policy options to reduce FHA's exposure to risk from its program to guarantee single-family mortgages, including creating a larger role for private lenders and restricting the availability of FHA's guarantees. The options are designed to let FHA continue to fulfill its primary mission of ensuring access to credit for first-time homebuyers and low-income borrowers. . . .

What Policy Options Did CBO Analyze?

Many changes have been proposed to reduce the cost of risk to the federal government from FHA's single-family mortgage guarantees. CBO analyzed illustrative versions of seven policy options, which generally represent the range of approaches that policymakers and others have proposed:

- Guaranteeing some rather than all of the lender's losses on a defaulted mortgage;

- Increasing FHA's use of risk-based pricing to tailor up-front fees to the riskiness of specific borrowers;

- Adding a residual-income test to the requirements for an FHA-insured mortgage to better measure borrowers' ability to repay the loan (as the Department of Veterans Affairs does in its mortgage guarantee program);

- Reducing the limit on the size of a mortgage that FHA can guarantee;

- Restricting eligibility for FHA-insured mortgages only to first-time homebuyers and low- to moderate-income borrowers;

- Requiring some borrowers to receive mortgage counseling to help them better understand their financial obligations; and

- Providing a grant to help borrowers with their down payment, in exchange for which FHA would receive part of the increase in their home's value when it was sold.

Although some of those approaches would require action by lawmakers, several of the options could be implemented by FHA without legislation. In addition, certain options could be combined to change the nature of FHA's risk exposure or the composition of its guarantees. CBO did not examine the results of combining options.

Source: Options to Manage FHA's Exposure to Risk from Guaranteeing Single-Family Mortgages, Congressional Budget Office, September 2017, pp. 1–2.

you do your problem definition work well, you will end up with an important problem in your sights that in most cases can be mitigated to some degree by purposive action.

Another frequently helpful alternative is "Learn more." This can be done by using pilot studies, or by looking around for examples of "smart practices" elsewhere (see Part IV), or by waiting for the future to get less murky, or perhaps by negotiating further with important players to ascertain what they might do under various contingencies. Don't forget that there is a cost to waiting if, in the absence of further learning, you would have guessed "the right conclusion" anyway. Conversely, there is a cost to premature decision-making or action if you are likely to make a consequential mistake that could be corrected by further learning.

Model the System in Which the Problem Is Located

We often think about alternative approaches to the problem as possible *interventions* in the system that holds the problem in place or keeps it going. Logically, it is not necessary to model the causes of a problem in order to cure it—pharmaceutical manufacturers can testify that many of their successful products work by unknown causal routes on conditions whose causes are not at all understood. But a good causal model is often quite useful for suggesting possible "intervention points." This is especially true when the problem is embedded in a complex system of interacting forces, incentives, and constraints—which is usually the case.

Consider, for instance, a system that produces "too much traffic congestion" at some choke point such as a bridge or a tunnel. A sketch of the relevant causal model would include the demand for travel along the relevant route, the available alternative modes of travel, the amount of roadway capacity, and the price to users of roadway capacity. An efficient and simple—but usually politically unpopular—intervention might be to increase the price to users so as to reflect the degree to which each user contributes to congestion and increased travel times.

How self-conscious, elaborate, and rigorous should your causal model be? Many social scientists who devote themselves to policy analysis would hold, "The more so the better." We say, "Yes, but . . ." Self-consciousness is highly desirable. Elaborateness (or comprehensiveness—in this case a near synonym) is desirable because it decreases the risk of missing important causal connections, but it can blur the analytic focus and blunt creativity in designing intervention strategies. Rigor is desirable if it prevents you from relying on unarticulated and false assumptions; its downside is that it may persuade you to exclude factors that are important—for instance, the personalities of certain actors—because you don't know how to model their effect rigorously or because you have only hunches regarding the facts.

Many models are best thought of as elaborations of a fundamental metaphor. They can be mathematically precise or verbal and evocative. Some commonly used metaphors that are the bases for models of particular value in designing alternatives are discussed in the following sections.

Market Models. The model of a market in which disaggregated suppliers exchange goods or services with disaggregated demanders can apply to unpriced goods and services. The main idea behind the market model is really equilibration through exchange. Hence, the market model can be applied to many phenomena other than the production and allocation of textbook goods such as widgets or apples.

For instance, you might try to understand the flow of patients into a state mental hospital system in terms of supply and demand: there is a fixed short-run "supply" of available beds in state hospitals and a per-diem charge for each, and a complex "demand" for their use generated by police departments, county psychiatric emergency units, judges, members of the public, and so on.

A standard intervention strategy for improving markets that are not working as well as they might is to find some way to raise or lower the prices faced by either suppliers or demanders.

Production Models. Unfortunately, little academic literature has examined the operating logics of the common types of production systems found in public policy—such as command-and-control regulation, service provision, and all the others, which are briefly described in Appendix A, "Things Governments Do." (However, see Weimer and Vining 2011, chap. 10, on "generic policies"; see also Salamon 2002.) In any case, the main concern in understanding production systems should be to identify the parameters whose values, when they move out of a certain range, make the systems most vulnerable to breakdown, fraud and abuse, egregious diseconomies, and the distortion of intended purpose. It is also helpful to know about those parameters that matter most when we try to upgrade a production system from mere adequacy to performance levels we might think of as "excellent" (see Part IV, "'Smart (Best) Practices' Research").

Another way to look at production models is through optimization lenses. Operations research models—such as queuing, inventory management, and Markov processes—are relevant here.[11]

Conformity Models. Conformity models describe a process by which individuals adapt the attitudes and actions of other people around them. Psychologists have identified three sources of conformity: automatic mimicry and imitation, normative influence (doing what others do to increase social acceptance), and informational influence (the crowd is often a good source of information about what is correct or appropriate). An understanding of conformity models can improve the effectiveness of many interventions.

For instance, information policies intended to encourage healthier or more socially desirable behavior—such as posters hung on the walls of an inner-city school warning students of the dangers of dropping out—often fail to change behavior because they inadvertently reinforce the message that the "bad" behavior is prevalent—and people like to do what is "normal" for their reference group.

The key to designing more effective interventions is to leverage the tendency of people to think and act like people around them. For example, hotels have been able to significantly boost the percentage of guests who reuse bath towels (reducing water and energy use) by informing guests on signs in their rooms that reusing towels is a typical behavior of other hotel guests.

Evolutionary Models. An evolutionary model describes a common process of change over time. It is constructed of three important subprocesses: variation among competitors, selection, and retention. Suppose, for instance, that in an agency enforcing health-related standards in the workplace, the complaints disproportionately concerned visible and annoying problems that were not as hazardous to worker health as less visible and annoying problems. In this case, the evolutionary model suggests several plausible intervention points. The agency might try to educate workers to detect and complain about more serious problems, contriving thereby to swamp the less serious problems—thus changing the pool of "competitors." It might start screening the complaints for their likelihood of being associated with more fruitful targets—thus changing the "selection mechanism." Or it might attempt to persuade workers, and perhaps their union representatives, to reduce their propensity to complain about matters the agency wishes to hear less about—thus changing the "retention mechanism," workers' attitudes.[12]

Conceptualize and Simplify the List of Alternatives

The final list of alternatives—the one you include in your presentation to your client and other audiences—will almost certainly look quite different from the one you started with. Not only will you have thrown out some that just don't look very good, but you will also have done some work to *conceptualize* and *simplify* alternatives.

The key to conceptualization is to try to sum up the basic strategic thrust of an alternative in a simple sentence or even a phrase. This is difficult but usually worth the effort. It helps to use very plain, short phrases stripped of jargon. When the Environmental Protection Agency (EPA) was created, the first administrator confronted (a partial list of) alternatives that might have been described as thus: "Let the states do the work; let the feds give them the money"; "Remove impediments to firms cooperating on antipollution research"; and "Sue the bastards" (meaning the large, visibly polluting firms and industries, the prosecution of which would help build political support for the new agency).

The key to simplification is to distinguish between a basic alternative and its variants. The basic element in many policy alternatives is an intervention strategy—such as regulatory enforcement or a subsidy or a tax incentive—that causes people or institutions to change their conduct in some way.[13] But no intervention strategy can stand alone; it must be implemented by some agency or constellation of agencies (perhaps including nonprofit organizations), and it must have a source of financing. Usually the variants on the basic strategy are defined by different methods of implementation and different methods of financing.

The distinction between a basic strategy and variants based on implementation details is especially helpful when you have a lot of possible solutions to consider and you need to reduce the complexity involved in comparing them. Making the distinction puts you in a position to break your analysis into successive steps. In the first step, you might compare, say, three basic alternatives while ignoring the details described by their variants. Then, once you have decided on one of these basic alternatives, you could turn to comparing the variants.

For example, you want to decrease the prevalence of heroin use in your county by 50 percent over the next five years.[14] You consider three basic alternatives: methadone maintenance, law enforcement pressure, and drug education. Potential variants for each one have to do with the funding sources, in that state, federal, and county money can be used in different degrees (although not all mixes of funds available for one approach are also available for the other two). Variation is also possible according to who administers the program(s): nonprofit organizations, county employees, or state employees. Or you might consider variants of scale and scope, such as two possible sizes for your methadone program.

Points on a Continuum as "Alternatives"

Suppose you are asked to recommend changes in, say, the rental rates for public housing in your city. Theoretically, each penny change in the rent charged could represent an alternative, but clearly that is a mistaken way to consider "alternatives." A better approach is to make this into a two-step problem. Step one is to establish the upper and the lower limits of an acceptable range of possibilities, and step two is to choose some point within that range. Choosing each of these limits is a small policy problem in itself, complete with criteria, projections, and the like. For instance, equity might require that the upper limit not be "too high," meaning somewhere close to $600 per month, whereas affordability might suggest a slightly lower upper limit. Cost recovery requirements might suggest a lower limit of, say, $450 per month. In any case, suppose that at the end of step one, the acceptable range has been narrowed to $475–$575 per month. One might almost say that a good move for step two is simply to take the midpoint of these two limits, $525 per month. But there might be additional criteria of interest—for example, finding a "reasonable" increment relative to the current rental rate. If the current rate is $475 per month, a $50 increment, to $525, could be seen as reasonable, but so might a $75 increment (especially if rents have not been raised in several years), which will permit the city's housing authority to offer some needed services to residents. At any rate, $25 increments between $450 and $575 seem to be the psychologically "right" set of alternatives—not too large and not too small for the range of options to be considered. Thus, in the end, we have narrowed our alternatives down to six, from an initial array of several thousand.

This two-step procedure could be useful for a variety of problems involving near-continuous variables as alternatives—for example, budget allocations, future dates to begin or to discontinue a service, the number of people to be accommodated by some project or program, emission limits for some effluent, fee or fine schedules, or quantity of water to be released from a reservoir.

The great majority of social science hypotheses about what might work to ameliorate a given problem show up in the language of continuous variables, which then need to be transformed by the policy analyst into policy-compatible discontinuous choices. If, for instance, studies show that the price elasticity of a pack of cigarettes is −.4, that tells you about a continuous relationship (within a certain range) between aggregate cigarettes demanded and the price charged. But if you want to exploit this fact to raise cigarette taxes so as to discourage smoking, you need to translate this information into particular numbers—for example, "Raise the tax $0.25 per pack to $1.75."

Alternatives Should Be Detailed

A recurring question is how detailed to be in the characterization of "an alternative," especially in the early stages of one's work.

The usual answer should be "more detailed," since there is a natural reluctance to commit oneself to particulars, especially if one is likely to change one's mind eventually anyway. Detail supports clearer thinking—and also clearer communication with others. The more detail, the less room for talking past one another or for agreeing (disagreeing) when, given the underlying interests and the realistic scope for action, the parties are simply disguising their differences from each other and, probably, from themselves.

Actually, it is a certain kind of detail that is most valuable in characterizing alternatives: "behavioral" detail. Say what you expect people to actually be doing, and especially what you expect them to be doing differently from what is being done now. For instance, "Increase facility inspections from one per year to two or more per year." Or, "Abolish about half the current safety net features now provided in kind in favor of giving cash."

These arguments for more detail, particularly more behavioral detail, also apply to Step One: Define the Problem.

Multistage Analysis

Most of this book focuses on a "one-off" decision (and/or design) process that has a beginning, middle, and end. However, many policy choices are—or should be—part of a process. A single choice is not once-and-for-all but part of a developmental sequence of choices mixed with developments unfolding in the policy environment.

This possibility should show up in one's thinking about the construction of alternatives. Here are some common process-based alternatives.

There is the classic "wait and see" version. The first decision in this process is to let present trends continue and then to monitor what happens as a result. The second decision comes at some time later, to be made in light of what has happened in the interim.

Another version of multistage analysis is contingency planning: "X or Y will (probably) occur. We will wait until that is resolved. If X, then we should choose A; if Y, then we should choose B." For example, the Department of Homeland Security might take certain steps to protect the nation's ports if a threat of a terrorist attack is made, and then take additional steps if a detailed security assessment finds that the threat is indeed credible.

A third version turns on political feasibility. Political feasibility is not only a condition to be assessed; it is a challenge to be addressed, and addressed in such a way as to help shape a group's choices about policy. The simple version is begin to form a political coalition around a problem or objective, and see what policy options find most favor with the emergent coalition. For more details about such a process, see Appendix C, "Strategic Advice on the Dynamics of Gathering Political Support."

Fourth, there is learning by doing. A reasonable policy choice is to start small and easy, make some mistakes along with some successes, learn from both mistakes and successes, and scale up over a few years. Arrangements can even be made for systematic evaluation, either at the beginning or later in the evolution of the policy. Unfortunately, this strategy is better in theory than in practice, since changing political environments and personnel turnover make social learning both hard to do and hard to institutionalize.

STEP FOUR: SELECT THE CRITERIA

It helps to think of any policy story (see Step Eight) as having two interconnected but separable plotlines, the analytic and the evaluative. The first is all about facts and disinterested projections of consequences, whereas the second is all about value judgments. Ideally, all analytically sophisticated and open-minded persons can agree, more or less, on the rights and wrongs in the analytic plotline and on the nature of its residual uncertainties. But this is not true with regard to the evaluative plotline—where we expect subjectivity and social philosophy to have freer play. The analytic plotline will reason about whether X, Y, or Z is likely to happen, but it is in the evaluative plotline that we learn whether we think X or Y or Z is good or bad for the world.

This fourth step in the Eightfold Path belongs primarily, though not exclusively, to the evaluative plotline. It is the most important step for introducing values and philosophy into the policy analysis, because some possible "criteria" are evaluative standards used to judge the goodness of the projected policy outcomes that are associated with each of the alternatives.

Of course, the most important evaluative criterion is whether or not the projected outcome will solve the policy problem to an acceptable degree. But this is only the beginning. After all, any course of action is likely to affect the world in many ways, some desired and some not. Each of those effects—or projected outcomes, to apply our Eightfold Path language—requires a judgment on your part as to whether or not, and why or not, it is thought desirable. Our set of criteria embodies such judgments. Because any significant impact cries out for such a judgment to be made, the greater the variety of significant impacts, the richer will be the set of evaluative criteria needed to deal with them.

Semantic Tip Evaluative criteria are not used to judge the *alternatives*, at least not directly. They are to be applied to the projected *outcomes.* It is easy to get confused about this point—and to get the analysis very tangled as a result. This confusion is encouraged by a commonsense way of speaking: "Alternative A looks to be the best; therefore, let's proceed with it." But this phrasing ignores a very important step. The complete formulation is "Alternative A will very probably lead to Outcome O_A, which we judge to be the best of the possible outcomes; therefore, we judge Alternative A to be the best." Applying criteria to the evaluation of outcomes and not of alternatives makes it possible to remember that we might like O_A a great deal even if, because we lack sufficient confidence that A will actually lead to O_A, we decide not to choose Alternative A after all. With that judgment on the table, it will be possible to look for other alternatives with a greater likelihood of producing O_A.

Commonly Used Evaluative Criteria

Hit the Target! We sometimes want, or need, to achieve a particular goal by a particular date—for example, cut the rate of state water consumption by 5 percent for the first quarter of next year. Or de-lead all painted interior surfaces in a certain neighborhood by December 31 of this year. Stipulating such concrete targets is often useful for political purposes like mobilizing resources and focusing attention, but it can also be very helpful in framing an analytic agenda. The target might originate in a political mandate, or it might simply be an invented analytic construct. If it is the latter, revisiting the target during the course of the analysis might prove necessary, as the initial version is eventually likely to look too high or too low.

Efficiency. Typically, the efficiency criterion is the most important evaluative consideration in cost-effectiveness and benefit–cost studies. We use *efficiency*, more or less as the term is used in economics, for maximizing the aggregate of individuals' welfare as that welfare would be construed by the individuals themselves—in economic jargon, "Maximize the sum of individual utilities," or "Maximize net benefits." Another roughly equivalent formulation would be "Maximize the public interest."

Although *efficiency* has an antiseptic, technocratic, and elitist ring to it, the insistence here that "utilities" are to be assessed according to individual citizens' construction of their own welfare is thoroughly democratic. Indeed, siding with efficiency—on average, across most policy issues and policy decisions—is a way to produce more humanistic policy results, too. The reason is not that efficiency is so very humane a concept in itself, but that policy decisions failing to consider efficiency very often fail to take account of the welfare of the little guy at all. The little guy may be little, but in a proper efficiency analysis, he at least shows up to be counted. Efficiency analysis imposes a moral check (for whatever that is worth in the real world of politics) on political visionaries eager to relocate entire populations so as to make room for dams, and on special interests eager to impose seemingly small price increases on large numbers of consumers through protectionist measures in order to maintain the incomes of a relatively small number of producers.

We should observe, though, that from the point of view of social justice, the efficiency criterion may be somewhat limited. First, because analysts typically estimate people's "utility" by inferring their willingness to pay for some benefit (or to be spared some deprivation), individuals with less money do not, in an analytic sense, have as much clout as those with more. Just how big a limitation this analytic anti-egalitarianism turns out to be will depend on particular cases, however. Second, if the values at stake have few or no human defenders, and therefore no human pocketbooks to back an estimate of willingness to pay, the efficiency criterion may underestimate these values even if by some conception of justice they ought to be weighted heavily. In theory, environmental values are the main example, although in fact some environmental values do have human defenders who derive enormous utility from preserving them—a utility that would be accounted for in a proper efficiency analysis.

Although cost-effectiveness analysis and benefit–cost analysis sound alike and are frequent traveling companions, they are not the same, and their uses can be quite different. True, both construe the policy problem as involving some production relationship between resources and objective(s). And both entail thinking about the relationship by using an economizing lens. However, cost-effectiveness analysis is usually satisfied to assess how well a policy achieves the nature and quantity of the desired outputs,[15] whereas benefit–cost analysis goes a step further and tries to evaluate how much those outputs are valued in terms of money or (rarely) actual utility by individuals. Because it is less ambitious, the cost-effectiveness approach is more common in policy analysis than is the benefit–cost approach.[16] Indeed, a surprisingly large number of policy issues can be simplified and stylized as cost-effectiveness problems, even though on the surface they may not appear to be likely candidates at all for this sort of treatment. Here are two examples:

- The Mudville mayor wishes to respond to business complaints that building permits "take forever" to obtain. Given that you can spend no more than $500 and are permitted to change the workflow in the city planning office but not personnel assignments, the cost-effectiveness framework might suggest minimizing delay (measured in days) arising from purely procedural and bureaucratic sources.

- Quake City must upgrade the seismic safety of several thousand buildings constructed of unreinforced masonry. You have a twenty-year time span and no immediate budget constraint, but you wish to accomplish the job with minimum disruption to the lives (and incomes) of the residents and small businesses that may be displaced temporarily by the building renovation process. To minimize such disruption, cost-effectiveness analysis might lead you to propose that the work be done in one season rather than another, or that not all grocery stores be closed at once, or that tenants be assisted in organizing mutual-aid groups. A variant of this is that you have a target deadline (see above) and a budget constraint, and you want to find the most cost-effective means of achieving the target while staying within the constraint.

Relative to the benefit–cost approach, a cost-effectiveness framework typically simplifies policy analysis in another useful way, as well: It assumes as *fixed* either resources or outputs, and focuses only on choices involving the other member of this pair. Fixed resources usually involve a money budget or a human or physical asset such as a work team or a set of hospital beds. A fixed output is generally a target of some kind, such as a minimum required pollution abatement level or a maximum acceptable proportion of children failing an achievement test. Analysis then involves finding the best means to manipulate the other member of the cost-effectiveness pair so as to improve productive efficiency. Colloquially, if resources are fixed, you are "getting the biggest bang for the buck," or if you have a fixed target, you may be "doing no worse with less."

Now suppose that, once you have figured out some approach whereby you can do no worse with less, you want to broaden your inquiry to explore whether you can make use of this new and better approach to produce a little (or even a lot) more than you had originally planned. That is, instead of assuming that either resources or outputs are fixed, you are prepared to allow the scale of the activity to increase. The analytic challenge is much more difficult now, because at this point you cannot avoid the question of whether the augmented output "is worth it," given the envisioned cost increment. That question cannot be answered unless you compare the utilities of *both* the cost increment and the augmented output. That is, cost-effectiveness analysis must now rise to the level of benefit–cost analysis.[17]

Here is an excerpt of a 2005 RAND Corporation benefit–cost analysis— concerning the social return on investing in universal preschool in California. The study reached these conclusions:

- Using our preferred assumptions, a one-year high-quality universal pre-school program in California is estimated to generate about $7,000 in net present value benefits per child for California society (public and private sectors) using a 3 percent discount rate. This equals a return of $2.62 for every dollar invested, or an annual rate of return of about 10 percent over a sixty-year horizon.

- Assuming a 70 percent participation rate in the universal preschool pro-gram, each annual cohort of California children served generates $2.7 billion in net present value benefits to California society (using a 3 percent discount rate).

- These estimates from our benefit–cost model are sensitive to assumptions about the distribution of benefits that accrue to more- and less-disadvantaged children from participating in a high-quality preschool program. When we consider a range of assumptions from the more conservative to the less conservative (where our baseline results above fall in between), we find that California is estimated to gain at least two dollars for every dollar invested and possibly more than four dollars.[18]

Equality, Equity, Fairness, Justice. There are, of course, a great many dif-ferent, and often opposed, ideas about what these terms do, or should, mean. In addition to thinking hard about these ideas yourself, sometimes you should also take your audience through some of that thinking, as in the following examples:

- Drivers who do not carry liability insurance leave persons whom they injure in auto accidents at risk of being undercompensated. Many of those who "go bare" are relatively poor. Many other drivers purchase their own insurance against exactly this risk ("uninsured-motorist coverage"). A policy proposal to pay for all drivers' liability insurance out of a fund created by surcharges at the fuel pump was denounced by some observers as "inequitable" to the poor, who were going bare of insurance. Other observers said that those who go bare impose inequitable premium expenses or risks of undercompensation on the rest of society, including many individuals who are poor or not very well off. Clearly, the analyst needs to include a discussion of the idea of equity.

- The current debate over whether to retain affirmative action preferences for African Americans and certain other minorities in university admissions is sometimes said to pit fairness to individuals against justice to social groups. This is odd, though, since some philosophers—and most ordinary folk, too—suppose that no system claiming to be just could contain any features deemed unfair. Again, the analyst has a job to do in sorting out ideas and language.

Freedom, Community, and Other Ideas. To stimulate thought, here is a (far from complete) list of more ideas of possible relevance as evaluative criteria: free markets, economic freedom, capitalism, "freedom from government control," equality before the law, equality of opportunity, equality of result, free speech, religious freedom, privacy, safety (especially from chemicals, various environmental hazards, and the like), neighborliness, community, sense of belonging, order, security, absence of fear, traditional family structure, egalitarian family structure, empowerment of workers, maintenance of a viable nonprofit sector, voluntarism, and trust in others.

Process Values. American democracy values process and procedure—that is, having a say in policy issues that affect you, rationality, openness and accessibility, transparency, fairness, and nonarbitrariness—as well as substance. These considerations probably apply to the very design or decision process for which you are doing your present analytic work. Therefore, remember to consult broadly and equitably. In addition to building up legitimacy for your work, you may be surprised at how much you can learn, especially from people who are very unlike yourself socially or ideologically. This does not, of course, mean that you should in the end accord equal deference to all opinions or desires, or keep the consultative process open forever. Some opinions are more creditable than others, and at some point consultation must give way to decision.

Do not make the mistake of thinking that "more participation" or "greater access to the process" necessarily equates to "more democratic" or "more rational." Greater opportunities for participation may be exploited more heavily by those with more time to participate or by those with special interests to protect or by ideological zealots. Ordinary people and their ordinary concerns can come out as relative losers.

Some Evaluative Criteria
Deserve More Weight Than Others

As we saw in the case of defining the problem, when values are at issue—as they are in regard to criterion selection, as well—we must reckon how to weight opposing values. There are three general approaches to this problem.

The Political Process Takes Care of It. One approach is simply to allow existing governmental and political processes to determine the weighting. Typically, this approach will accord primacy to the analyst's employer or client, as well as allowing derivative influence to be exercised by those parties in the relevant arena who are in turn important to the employer or client.

The Analyst Imposes a Solution. A second approach is for the analyst herself to modify—though not replace—the weighting assigned by the employer or client by reference to some overarching philosophical or political conception. The justification usually offered for this approach is that because certain interests, and perhaps philosophies, are typically "underrepresented" in government and politics, and because the analyst is in a better position than most other participants in the process to see or understand or appreciate this problem of underrepresentation, the analyst is duty-bound, or at least permitted, in the name of fairness and democracy, to right the balance.

For instance, some observers would argue that were it not for policy analysts, efficiency-related criteria would rarely be heeded and that, as a consequence, analysts should in effect speak up for the taxpayers whose interests may be squeezed out by better-organized advocacy groups. A related argument is sometimes made that certain conceptions of equity—in particular those having to do with the idea that the beneficiaries of publicly provided goods or services should pay for them—are underrepresented except among policy analysts. (These conceptions of equity typically exclude public expenditures deliberately intended to redistribute wealth among citizens.) Other interests that people sometimes claim are underrepresented and therefore need representation by analysts are future generations, children, people who live outside the jurisdiction making the decisions, ethnic and racial minorities, women, the poor, consumers, and animals and plants (ecological entities).

A variant of this approach introduces the idea of an educational process. Depending on circumstances, the analyst might encourage influential political actors—perhaps including the analyst's boss or principal client—to rethink their existing criteria in the light of facts or arguments the analyst can draw to their attention. In this case, the analyst takes responsibility for opening up a dialogue, and perhaps for trying to infuse it with reason and insight, but then allows the political process to take over.

The analyst can help the dialogue along by making sure that the assigning of weights will be done in the context of confronting the trade-offs, and framed as crisply and clearly as possible. (See "Step Six, Confront the Trade-Offs.") For instance, "We project that a choice of Route A for the railroad will impose $20 million more in construction costs than a choice of Route B. Route A is five miles longer than Route B (which is about 2 percent); however, Route A will permit us to spare the homes of about thirty families, half of whom have lived in the area for at least ten years. We are offering a $300,000-per-family compensation if they have to move, and twenty of the families seem willing to do that. But that still leaves ten families who might be unhappy with this solution. So a lot of your decision here probably rests on just how much weight you give to imposing on these ten families versus saving the $20 million in construction costs."

The Distribution of "Rights" Precludes Some Solutions and Forwards Others. If X has a recognized property "right," you can't easily override it just because your policy solution would find that convenient; and if Y has a "right" to privacy, you might be inclined to tilt the weighting of criteria heavily in that direction. Generally, claims based on rights are a reasonable guide to choosing "better" policies, and rights-based criteria deserve some extra weighting. However, plenty of exceptions exist, and it pays to examine, briefly, the whole matter of where rights come from and how policy analysis can make good use of them. This is a controversial matter, of course, and our thoughts on it are certainly contestable.

Typically, rights are specially protected claims of an individual or a group against encroachment by "others," including society as a whole, though in some cases it is society that claims the rights against component groups or individuals. Sometimes rights are long-standing, well established, consensual, and, within our social context, unquestioned, as in "X has a right to be treated with dignity, irrespective of X's economic condition." In these cases, the pattern of rights claims, hedged and limited though they might be, very likely is found to be a good self-help tool for organizing the many and varied interactions in a complex society. But rights are sometimes more emergent than established, and claims based on rights can be quite contentious or in conflict: "I have a right to use my cell phone in any place, private or public," versus "I have a right not to be disturbed by your loud and obnoxious cell phone conversation, thank you very much."

It is best to think of *all* rights claims as emerging from a social process of trial and error and contestation, with the ones that seem obviously legitimate to us being merely the (so far) best established and (probably) most socially beneficial. Claims that particular rights are justified by nature or "divine will" or reason or "our common humanity" are simply rhetoric, because these justifications are always challenged by others. Over the centuries through which these debates have continued, no permanent resolution has occurred, and we think one will never occur, since rights are simply convenient tools of social organization and rights-based claims a consensually accepted way of negotiating the changing landscape of whose interests should be protected to what degree and with what exceptions.

From the point of view of a hypothetical social engineer trying to improve social welfare, some rights should certainly be treated as relatively fundamental. If the moral realm were the legal realm, these rights would be considered constitutional. But, like the Constitution, even fundamental rights, such as "the right to privacy" or "the right to control your own body," should evolve to fit new social and technological conditions. Technological change raises questions of privacy and transparency (e.g., confidentiality and fairness), and the past structure of rights is not necessarily a good guide to how to redesign that structure for the emergent situation. A fortiori, this applies to matters of lesser moment—where it is easier to see that rights are constructed rather than found. Forcing others to listen to your cell phone conversation may or may not be a right we wish to create and honor, but it is surely novel, and it needs to be settled by reference not to reason and the like but rather to the balancing of utilities in a strictly pragmatic fashion. The same applies to compensation for takings, decent health care, privacy, abortion, and a host of other matters that now or in the recent past have been subject to debate over who ought to have what sort of highly protected positions that we dignify and crystallize as rights.

Please do not misunderstand this as an argument in favor of relativism, which in many people's usage is the same as saying that there is no choosing among different rights claims, that one is as good as another. That is not true. Certainly, allowing people to claim a high level of protection for (i.e., a right to) certain values—such as individual autonomy—is beneficial to the running of a modern democratic society. But this right sometimes needs to have exceptions carved out of it to accommodate cases when the exercise of this right imposes excessively on other people. The fine texture of the fabric of such rights is always subject to discussion, and the basis for making these decisions is to be found not in rhetoric or in philosophical speculation but in the analysis of alternative fabrics, each taken as a whole and including all the internal tensions that are bound to be included in them. The evolution of rights in the moral realm—that is, in the realm of private practice and thence public opinion formation—involves the sort of constant tinkering and adjustment we see in the realm of both statutory and judge-made law.

In the end, therefore, claims to weight criteria by reference to which rights ought or ought not to take priority deserve to be treated critically.

Commonly Used Practical Criteria

Not all criteria that come into play in an analysis are part of the evaluative plotline. Some are purely practical and are part of the analytic plotline. These criteria have to do with what happens to an alternative as it moves through the policy adoption and policy implementation processes.[19] The main ones are legality, political acceptability, administrative robustness and improvability, and policy sustainability.

Legality. A feasible policy must not violate constitutional, statutory, or common law rights. Remember, however, that legal rights are constantly changing and are often ambiguous. It is sometimes worth taking a gamble on a policy that might—or might not—be adjudged illegal when tested in court. (In such cases, advice of counsel is clearly in order to help craft the policy so that its survival chances are enhanced.)

Semantic Tip   As noted above, however, remember that rights alleged to be "natural" or "human" are conceptually quite different from legal rights, despite the semantic similarity. Examples are the conflicting abortion stances predicated on right-to-life values or a woman's right to control her own body. Alleged natural or human rights are sometimes controversial in that some people would like to have them recognized as legal prescriptions whereas others would oppose such recognition.

Political Acceptability. A feasible policy must be politically acceptable, or at least not unacceptable. Political unacceptability is a combination of two conditions: too much opposition (which may be wide or intense or both) and/or too little support (which may be insufficiently broad or insufficiently intense or both) for the proposal to win adoption.

A stakeholder analysis can help gauge political acceptability. First, using web searches, interviews, and other research methods, identify the relevant actors—including elected and appointed officials, businesses, trade associations, professional societies, advocacy groups, and ideological organizations—that might plausibly take a stand (pro or con) on the proposal. Keep in mind that actors are more likely to become active if they have been involved with an issue in the past, if they believe a proposal impinges on their interests or ideological goals, and if they perceive that they will bear losses under the proposal (people tend to react more strongly to losses than to gains of equal size).

. Too little support
. Too much opposition

Second, list the resources possessed by each actor, such as authority, expertise, financial resources, and the ability to mobilize or speak on behalf of others.

Finally, identify the institutional venues in which decisions will be considered, the rules and procedures by which each such venue operates, and the type of claims each venue permits to be heard (e.g., courts require parties to have "legal standing" and to express their preferences in terms of duties and rights).

Do not take a static view of political unacceptability, however. Always ask yourself the question, "If my favorite policy solution doesn't look acceptable under current conditions, what would it take to change those conditions?"

You may discover that creative political strategizing can change the set of relevant stakeholders, modify their respective preferences or resources, or shift the institutional context in which policies will be made, thereby opening up options that haven't been seriously considered before. (Discussion of techniques for building coalitions and launching successful campaigns is far beyond the scope of this book, but Appendix C, "Strategic Advice on the Dynamics of Gathering Political Support," sketches some of the basics.)

In assessing strategic limitations and possibilities, it will help to make use of various models of the political process. As we observed earlier, models are based on metaphors, and the ones that are likely to be most valuable in this case are these:

- A game in which strategic actors (both individuals and groups) seek to maximize their payoffs without cheating, given both the rules of the game and the strategic behavior of the other players[20]

- A war, in which partisan or ideological armies seek to defeat and demoralize their political enemies, preserve past victories, and conquer new policy territory

- A theater, in which the actors are elected officials who strive, with or without a basis in reality, to create a good appearance—to themselves, to each other, to the critics, and to the audience (whose approval, ultimately, is all-important)

- A marketplace of slogans, symbols, and ideas, with a mix of honorable merchants and hucksters as sellers and a mix of sophisticates and innocents as buyers

- A school in which elected officials learn how to do good policy design work and sometimes share their results and their methods with their classmates

How exactly is one to make use of such models? Think of them as conceptual lenses. Observe the relevant political process through each of them in turn, and identify the probable pitfalls and opportunities brought into focus by each.[21]

A common obstacle to the adoption of policies that would generate net benefits for society is that the changes will impose concentrated costs on the interest groups who profit from current arrangements. These clienteles will inevitably lobby against the proposals, and they may be better organized than the many people who would gain from the changes. By modifying the incidence of costs and benefits, however, it may be possible to boost the acceptability of a policy option without unduly blunting its effectiveness. Those who would bear losses under the policy might be given direct or indirect transitional assistance, for example. The use of "grandfather" clauses and "phase-ins" may also improve the odds of policy adoption.

Administrative Robustness and Improvability. Policy ideas that sound great in theory often fail under conditions of field implementation. The implementation process has a life of its own. It is acted out through large and inflexible administrative systems and is distorted by bureaucratic interests. It is also mediated by the incentives, preferences, and capacities of program "targets," such as low-income mothers who are required to participate in a "welfare-to-work" program.[22] Policies that emerge in practice can diverge, even substantially, from policies as designed and adopted. A policy alternative, therefore, should be robust enough that even if the implementation process does not go very smoothly, the policy outcomes will still prove to be satisfactory.

Some adverse implementation outcomes usually worth worrying about are long delays; excessive budgetary or administrative costs; scandal from fraud, waste, and abuse that embarrasses supporters; and administrative complexities that leave citizens (and program managers) uncertain as to what benefits are available or what or how regulations must be complied with.

Even the best policy planners cannot get all the details right at the design stage. They should therefore allow room for policy implementers to improve on the original design. The most common vehicle for such improvement is participation in the implementation process by individuals and groups whose expertise or point of view was not included in the design phase. However, the openness that makes for improvability can also, by opening the door to hostile political interests, diminish robustness. Hence, a careful evaluation of the current factual situation—personalities, institutional demands and incentives, political vulnerabilities, and so on—is usually in order.

In estimating robustness and improvability, models of bureaucracy can serve as useful conceptual lenses, as suggested earlier with regard to carrying out political analysis. We find the most useful metaphors for bureaucracy to be these, listed in no particular order:

- An automaton enacting preprogrammed routines ("standard operating procedures," or "SOPs")

- A person in an environment, driven by survival needs, self-enhancement interests, and, under some conditions, a desire for self-actualization

- A political arena wherein individuals and factions jockey for influence over the organization's mission, access to its decision systems, and its prerequisites

- A tribe with its own rituals and an array of safeguards against contamination by "outsiders"

- A society of individuals cooperating toward a more-or-less common set of goals

- A structure of roles and interrelationships that are intended to complement one another in a rational division of labor

- An instrument used by "society" for society's own objectives

Policy Sustainability. Policies typically must endure for a period of time to achieve their desired impacts, but the elected officials who voted for the policies will not remain in office forever, and their successors may have different agendas. Moreover, the groups who opposed a policy's adoption may return to fight another day. Rather than a one-shot affair, policymaking is a *dynamic* process in which the consolidation of a new policy may be more challenging than winning its adoption in the first place. Sustainability refers to the capacity of a policy to outlast its enacting coalition, maintain its integrity, and deploy core principles to stave off unwarranted political pressures for debilitating changes.

Policies "stick" not simply because they produce net social benefits but also because they generate "enough" support from key constituencies over time. The most durable policies create "positive feedback" by encouraging citizens, businesses, and groups to adjust to the new reality. Once that happens, such actors become reluctant to have the policy repealed or fundamentally changed, because they want to protect their investments in the new ways of doing things. Social Security's history illustrates these dynamics. When Social Security was created in 1935, the elderly were the least active age group in politics. As Social Security grew, it built a constituency among senior citizens by "(a) giving them the resources of money and free time; (b) enhancing their levels of political interest and efficacy by tying their well-being visibly to a government program; and (c) creating incentives for interest groups to mobilize them by creating a political identity based on program recipiency."[23] Durable policies not only build supportive clienteles and shape social identities. They also divide opponents in ways that make policy reversal more difficult.

Some sustainability risks to be concerned about include initial passage by a thin or temporary majority; lack of bipartisan support; benefit flows that are too small, too delayed, too uncertain, too invisible, or too stigmatizing to mobilize supporters and encourage self-reinforcing adaptations; capture of program benefits by a relatively underserving or unintended group; and lack of credibility of the government's commitment to the policy.[24]

"Criteria" as Logical Constructs

Criteria such as efficiency, equity, political acceptability, and robustness are substantive. But we can think of criteria of a purely formal sort, as well. For instance, we can distinguish among criterion values that we wish to maximize, those that must be minimally satisfied, and those of a generally lesser priority for which "more is better."

It is helpful to focus initially on one primary criterion, a *principal objective to be maximized* (or minimized). Typically, this principal objective will be the obverse of your problem definition. For instance, if your problem is that too many families are homeless, then your principal objective will probably be to minimize the number of homeless families. If the problem is that global temperatures are rising too rapidly, a good statement of a principal objective might be "Minimize or reverse the increase of global temperatures." Naturally, there are other criteria to judge outcomes by, such as costliness, political acceptability, and economic justice, and these should all enter into the final evaluation. However, unless you focus—initially, at least—on a single primary criterion and array others around it, you will likely find yourself getting very confused. As you get deeper into the analysis and feel more comfortable with a multiplicity of important objectives, you may wish to drop your emphasis on a primary criterion and work on a more complex "objective function," in the language of mathematical programming. See Box I-5 for an example of selecting the criteria from a real-world report.

Linear Programming. A mathematical (and now computer-accessible) technique for optimizing choice when you have a principal objective or an objective function and a scarce stock of resources for maximizing it is called "linear programming."[25] Often, at least some of the resources—such as the agency budget and the available physical facilities promised by a nonprofit agency—are constrained. Even if the problem is not subject to simple quantitative assessment, analysts often find it useful to take advantage of the logical structure of linear programming to conceptualize their task. The conventional formulation then sounds like this: "Maximize this objective (or objective function) subject to such-and-such resource constraints."

Box I-5 An Illustrative Example of "Selecting the Criteria" from a Policy Analysis Report

From: *Alternative Approaches to Funding Highways*, Congressional Budget Office, March 2011, vii, 9–10, https://www.cbo.gov/sites/default/files/112th-congress-2011-2012/reports/03-23-highwayfunding.pdf

Approaches to funding highways can be evaluated in terms of equity and economic efficiency. Equity, or fairness, is subjective and can be assessed in several ways. Observers of highway funding often gauge fairness by considering the share of funding that is obtained from taxes paid by highway users rather than from general taxpayer funds, from people in households that fall into various income categories, or from people in rural versus urban households.

The economic efficiency of a funding approach depends partly on its effects on users' travel behavior and partly on what it costs to implement. Charging users for the costs their travel imposes on society would create incentives for people to limit highway use to trips for which the benefits exceed the costs, thus reducing or eliminating overuse of highways and helping identify the economic value of investments in highways. However, the costs of collecting and enforcing such user charges also must be considered in evaluating their net effect on efficiency. . . .

Equity

The equity implications of fuel taxes, the primary current source of HTF [Highway Trust Fund] revenues, are mixed: Fuel taxes satisfy the user-pays criterion, but they tend to be regressive; that is, they impose a larger relative burden on low-income than on high-income households. An analysis of 2004 data on effective tax rates (taxes paid divided by income) that divided all households into five groups of equal size by income showed that people whose households were in the second-lowest and middle quintiles paid somewhat larger shares of their income in gasoline taxes than did people in the lowest quintile or in the top two quintiles (see Table 3 on page 14). Fuel taxes are less directly burdensome for households in the bottom group of earners, in part because people in some of those households do not own automobiles. However, the diesel fuel tax also imposes an indirect burden (which is not reflected in the table) through the effect on the prices of shipped goods. Because lower-income households consume larger shares of their income, that indirect effect would add to the overall regressivity of the fuel taxes considered together.

(Continued)

(Continued)

Some observers find another equity concern in the fact that fuel taxes disproportionately affect people who live in rural areas. According to data from the Department of Transportation's National Household Travel Survey, people in rural households spend more, on average, on gasoline or diesel fuel because their vehicles (including light-duty trucks and older cars) tend to be less fuel efficient than are the vehicles of their urban counterparts and because people in rural areas tend to drive more. The survey data indicate that rural households at all income levels spend more on gasoline and diesel fuel than is spent by comparable urban or suburban households. For example, rural households with income below $25,000 spent 30 percent more than did their urban counterparts, in part because they drove 13 percent more miles. Relative differences in spending on fuel between rural and urban households were even greater among other income groups.

Efficiency

In terms of efficiency, two aspects of fuel taxes are positive: First, the costs of collection and enforcement are low, in part because fuel taxes are not collected directly from individual service stations or from users of fuel but from fuel distributors, which collect them from the service stations where the money is collected from fuel purchasers. (In 2008, there were 114,000 filling stations and about 8,000 distributors in the United States.) Second, in combination with state and local fuel taxes, the federal taxes give motorists an incentive to reduce fuel consumption, thereby reducing the external costs associated with that consumption and, to some extent, the costs related to mileage.

[Footnotes, tables and references to the tables omitted from excerpt.]

Source: *Alternative Approaches to Funding Highways.* Congressional Budget Office, 2011.

Here is an example from the homelessness problem: "Maximize the number of homeless individuals housed on any given night, subject to the constraints of not exceeding $50,000 per-night total budgetary cost to Agency X, not putting shelters into Neighborhoods A and B for political reasons, and trying to give 'more' choice to the beneficiary population as to where they will take shelter."

Semantic Tip   If it is possible to sort your criteria according to whether they refer to values to be maximized or minimized, values that stand as constraints, or values that have a more-is-better or less-is-better quality, keep the different statuses of the criteria in mind. Be conscious of them. You can do this with a simple verbal trick: As appropriate, define your criteria as "maximize such-and-such value," "satisfy such-and-such value constraint," or "minimize such-and-such value." For example, minimize tons of carbon dioxide (CO_2) released; or maximize lives saved per dollar spent. If a criterion label contains no signal as to the better direction to move in, as in "governance structure" or "effect on landlords," it is almost certainly insufficient.

In any case, to the extent possible, the criteria should be characterized both in conceptual and in operational (typically quantitative) terms. Conceptually, for instance, one talks about "maximizing the reduction of greenhouse gas emissions from publicly owned buildings," whereas operationally, one talks about "minimizing the tons of greenhouse gas emissions per month from publicly owned buildings." In this case, the operational definition is a close proxy for the more qualitative conceptual definition. Frequently, however, something of a gap exists, since what is measurable may only imperfectly reflect the conceptual characterization. For instance, minimizing "the hassle factor" to the citizen in recycling his garbage is conceptually meaningful but hard to express quantitatively. It is really about the psychology of effort, the degree of belief in the desirability of the goal, and the degree of frustration involved in preparing one's garbage for pickup. In this case, the best you could probably manage operationally would be to estimate the number of minutes the citizen spends per week to cooperate in the enterprise.

To the extent possible, group your criteria in such a way that all the "positive" (benefit) criteria are clustered separately from the "negative" (cost) criteria. In a logical sense, how one does this does not really matter. But it makes for easier reading and discussion. It is a little like arranging your bridge hand by suit and, within suits, by number sequence.

Don't embrace euphemisms or other dodges as a substitute for words that describe harsh realities. The client for one student project asked for advice on what adult school programs to cut in order to save money in financially desperate circumstances. The students initially put together a brief defending adult school programming in general, at best leaving to inference what elements of the bundle were most deserving of cuts.

Specify Metrics

Clarity about criteria is greatly helped by specifying metrics. Table I-1 illustrates this point. Qualitative framing of the criterion is stated in the left-hand column, and it is fairly clear. But aiming to specify the metrics that might give it additional meaning helps even more. In some cases, the addition of a metric also adds insight into what one really wants.

TABLE I-1

An Example of Metric Specification

Qualitative Description	Description with Quantitative Metrics
• Maximize postpartum accessibility to family planning	• Maximize number of prevented unwanted and unplanned pregnancies within the first x months after birth
• Maximize humane treatment of dairy cattle	• Maximize % of cows allowed to tend and raise offspring for at least x months after birth
• Minimize North Brookwood crime	• Bring burglary rate in North Brookwood down by 10% in next 12 months
• Minimize post-inspection carbon monoxide (CO) emissions from autos	• Minimize average tons of CO emissions from autos in 12 months post-inspection
• Satisfy political feasibility requirement	• Estimate odds >75% that governor will sign this executive order
• Lower implementation hassle	• Fewer hours spent persuading reluctant implementers

Note that the objective here is not to quantify but to clarify. Quantification is desirable when possible, and identifying a metric is a helpful step in doing so. But the real purpose here is to help your thinking.

Nor is the purpose at this stage to canvas data sources or figure out how data are to be collected and reported. That is important, but it is separate from trying to improve your thinking. In fact, for some metrics, you cannot imagine collecting data at all. In Table I-1, although you can imagine how you might collect data about burglary rates (row 3), collecting data about cows doing their maternal duty (row 2) seems a lot harder. And births prevented (row 1) is logically impossible, since the needed counterfactual does not exist. Indeed, this is true of all prevention programs; counterfactuals can at best be estimated, and only by looking at proxy measures and at the results of experiments with well-constructed control groups.

Avoid Confusing Alternatives and Criteria

Semantic Tip   *Alternatives* are courses of action, whereas *criteria* are mental standards for evaluating the results of action. How could you ever mistake an alternative for a criterion, or vice versa? As with many instances of confusion in policy analysis, the source of such a mistake is likely to be semantic. Consider, for example, a senior manager in a state regulatory agency dealing with worker safety. She wishes to incorporate worker complaints into the agency's strategy for targeting inspections across work sites in the state. Her assistant presents her with a number of alternatives for doing so, one of which is called "rapid-response (twenty-four-hour maximum) hotline." Not surprisingly, one of the criteria for assessing outcomes is "responsiveness." The alternative therefore seems a lot like the criterion. But this is an illusion. The alternative (course of action) is really the hotline. The main reason it looks like a criterion is that the *intention* of rapid response has crept into the definition of the alternative.[26] This is a dangerous mistake, because one should not assume through definition that an intention, as expressed in the verbal characterization of the alternative, will actually be realized.

This sort of confusion is most likely to arise when the internal activities of an organization are under discussion, since proposals to create or modify organizational units resonate with intentionality. Consider a proposal to create a performance measurement office, a strategic planning team, and a customer service department. The performance measurement office may end up, for whatever reasons, using meaningless measures collected by unreliable agents; the strategic planning team may be deliberately ignored by savvy or possibly unsavvy managers; and the customer service department may unintentionally end up as an instrument of customer alienation. We once questioned a student's proposal to create a "drug counseling service" for employees within an organization. The proposal seemed too weak to make a dent in the organization's problem. The student countered, "No, I'm talking about not just any old counseling service that might attack this problem, but an 'effective' one." Nothing in the student's account of how the service was to work increased the odds that it might really be effective. Effectiveness was assumed simply because the student wished to assume it.

STEP FIVE: PROJECT THE OUTCOMES

For each of the alternatives on your current list, project all the outcomes (or impacts) that you or other interested parties might reasonably care about. This is the hardest step in the Eightfold Path. Even veteran policy analysts do not usually do it very well. Not surprisingly, analysts often duck it entirely, disguising their omission by a variety of subterfuges. Hence, the most important advice about this step is simple: do it.

At least three great practical as well as psychological difficulties must be confronted here. First, "policy" is about the future, not about the past or the present, but we can never be certain about how the future will unfold, even if we engage it with the best of intentions and the most thoughtful of policy designs.

Second, "project the outcomes" is another way of saying, "be realistic." Yet realism is often uncomfortable. Most people prefer optimism. Policy can affect people's lives, fortunes, and sacred honor, for better or for worse. Making policy, therefore, imposes a moral burden heavier than many people care to acknowledge. Understandably, we would rather believe that our preferred or recommended policy alternative will accomplish what we hope and that it will impose fewer costs than we might realistically fear.

Third, there is what is sometimes called "the 51–49 principle." That is, in the thick of the policy fray, we are driven out of pure self-defense to treat 51 percent confidence in our projection as though it deserved 100 percent confidence, so that we sometimes mislead not only others but ourselves as well. The first difficulty—namely, that we can never have wholly convincing evidence about the future—compounds the second and third, inasmuch as our wishful thinking is not readily disciplined by reference to empirical demonstrations and proofs.

These psychological difficulties notwithstanding, systematic efforts to project outcomes are essential. For policymakers in a modern democracy, neither following gut instincts nor reading pigeon entrails is a responsible alternative.

Extend the Logic of Common Sense

In this section we discuss, in a very general way, the logic of combining models and evidence to produce usable projections of policy outcomes for the various alternatives being considered. The logic is largely that of common sense supported by social science methodology but with some important additions and subtractions.

First, policy analysis uses social science to the degree that it can. A great deal of social science is directed toward answering the question, "Is Model X of this piece of the world realistic?" Social scientific studies of this type can often be useful for diagnosing the existence of problems, mapping trends, and deciding whether some seemingly "smart" practice (see Part IV) is worth trying to replicate. You should be careful, however, to avoid using the social scientific standard of adequacy for judgments about the realism of a model, for it is quite conservative. In policy analysis, the looser, but more appropriate, standard should be whether reliance on a model can lead to better results and avoid worse results than less disciplined guesswork.

Second, policy analysis, as we have seen, uses multiple models. Most social science, in imitation of the hard sciences, looks for the "best" model (or, in the case of some practitioners, the "true" model). Because all models abstract from reality, however, even the best models are never complete. Although such abstraction may advance the progress of science, in the world of policy, where real consequences of policy choices are to be experienced by real people, no facet of a problem or the possible alternatives to be adopted can be exempted from analysis. Whatever models *can* be employed to illuminate some important facet of the problem or of the possible outcomes *should* be employed—even if doing so results in an inelegant and ad hoc multiplication of subanalyses.

Third, even when you have adopted adequately realistic models of sufficient number and variety, these models still need to be used in conjunction with evidence about "initial conditions," or the facts on the ground as they currently exist. For instance, "Deputy Director Smith is as incompetent as they come. The need to work around her will raise the risks of failure by at least 25 percent." Or, "The community appears very angry about the drug scene right now, and residents will almost certainly help the police in the planned crackdown." Although the projections of many models are not particularly sensitive to initial conditions, some are. These are the models that bear on projections of political acceptability and on the robustness of an alternative to the stresses of the implementation process.

Finally, policy analysis, as we have seen, makes use of the metaphors behind the models—metaphors such as "bureaucracy as automaton" and "politics as theater" and "this piece of the world as production system"—to yield qualitative insights about important causal relationships. The especially important relationships are those that may afford useful intervention points in complex systems or that present potential pitfalls in the policy adoption or implementation process.

Choose a Base Case

For the next step, "Confront the Trade-Offs," we counsel comparing the projected outcomes—the work of this present step—so that you can see clearly in what ways the various pairwise comparisons for which trade-offs exist differ from each other. This step, then, prepares the raw material for that next step. (See also the discussion of "setup for the next step," page 68.)

To do that, your projections should all be defined against a common reference mark, the *base case*. If the base case is whatever condition exists today, and that condition is not expected to change, then each outcome should be described in terms of the difference between what would (probably) exist tomorrow and what (arguably) exists today. For example, if poverty in Rivertown is 15 percent today, and Alternative A is expected to decrease it by, say, 2 percent, then the projected outcome is −2 percent or, in absolute numbers, 1,000 fewer individuals in poverty. If the comparable projection for Alternative B is −3 percent, or 1,500 fewer individuals in poverty, then it will be easy to see, when you come to confronting trade-offs, that B is better than A on this dimension by 500 fewer individuals in poverty. (It may also be more costly or less desirable in other ways, but those considerations can wait.)

If the base case is whatever condition exists today, and that condition *is* expected to change, then a comprehensive investigation could potentially be done of how the world will evolve in the absence of the adoption of each alternative under a particular condition. For example, federal agencies under President Obama were required to investigate the following baseline conditions to assess the impact of proposed regulatory changes: "the evolution of relevant markets; population or economic growth; possible behavioral changes, learning, and adaptation by relevant members of the public; technological changes and advances; and changes in regulations promulgated by the agency or other government entities."[27]

What is a good base case? Between the polar extremes of "whatever conditions exist today" and "how (multiple) present trends would unfold without the policy under consideration" are many other possibilities. Here is a list of some of them, along with a brief commentary:

- *Future conditions provided that business were to continue as usual.* The analysts whose conclusions on greenhouse gas abatement appear in Table I-2 chose this as their base case. They assumed no new regulations and no changes in fossil fuel consumption other than those caused by demographic changes. They did not include possible technological changes, for instance.

- *Changes from the present that would occur if some policy were to be adopted.* Suppose, for instance, that the state was likely to finance and construct a train system connecting major cities, and that this system was expected to reduce automobile usage overall by, say, 5 percent. This is like "business as usual" except that changes caused by a particular policy are in sharper focus.

- *Projections of the results of one particular policy option.* In 1996 the RAND Corporation, referred to earlier, published a study comparing the cost-effectiveness of crime reduction strategies programs to the base case of the "three-strikes" mandatory incarceration policy that California had recently adopted. Three out of the four programs were clearly more cost-effective, and the fourth possibly so. The objective was to show that on narrow crime-prevention grounds alone, and leaving aside humanistic considerations, three-strikes was wasting taxpayer money, since other options were cheaper for achieving the same objective.

It is worth noting that if the base case contains errors (from projecting the future or from misunderstanding the present), these will not matter if the errors do not affect the comparisons of the projected outcomes differently. In the example above, if the poverty rate in Rivertown is actually 16 percent rather than 15 percent, this mistake makes no difference if the absolute numbers of individuals projected to be helped are still 1,000 and 1,500.

TABLE I-2

Comparative Analysis: Anytown, USA (2050 baseline: 5.5 million metric tons CO_2e)

	Policy Scenario	(% reduction from 2050 CO_2e baseline) Efficacy	(Cost per ton CO_2e abated) Cost-Effectiveness	O (Operational) E (Economic) P (Political) Viability
EXISTING BUILDINGS	Mandate efficiency retrofits for homes	6.9% to 8.8%	–$130 to $5	O: High E: Medium P: High
	Mandate efficiency retrofits for commercial buildings	7.9% to 10.5%	–$132 to –$30	O: High E: Medium P: High
NEW BUILDINGS	Require zero-energy capable homes	4.1% to 5.6%	–$132 to –$25	O: High E: High P: High
	Require zero-energy capable commercial buildings	6.5% to 8.9%	–$120 to –$48	O: High E: High P: High
URBAN PLANNING	High-density residential development	2.4%	–$1,333 to –$702	O: High E: High P: Medium
ENERGY SUPPLY	Incentives for distributed PV	3.9%	$15 to $139	O: High E: Medium P: High
FINANCIAL MECHANISMS	$20 carbon tax	11.3%	$20	O: High E: Medium P: Low
	$50 carbon tax	20.6%	$50	O: High E: Medium P: Low

CO_2e = carbon dioxide emissions; PV = photovoltaic

Dare to Make Magnitude Estimates

Projecting outcomes often requires you to think not just about the general direction of an outcome but about its magnitude, as well. Typically it's not enough to say, "We expect this program to have a very positive effect on reducing unwanted teenage pregnancies." Instead, you would want to say, "We expect this program to reduce by one hundred to three hundred the number of unwanted teenage pregnancies per year in this community over the next five years." Developing magnitude estimates can help reduce the likelihood that an analysis will be misinterpreted. (If no numerical estimate is provided, policymakers may mistakenly assume the projected impact is zero. And if the projection really is zero, find a way to make that clear.)

Here is an example of a Congressional Budget Office (CBO) magnitude estimate of the impact of a bill (the Nutrition Reform and Work Opportunity Act of 2013) on participation in the Supplemental Nutrition Assistance Program (SNAP):

- "Section 109 would reduce the number of waivers available for certain childless adults who would otherwise be subject to work requirements or time limits. CBO estimates that, on average, about 1 million people with higher-than-average benefits would lose eligibility for SNAP benefits under this provision. The number of people losing benefits would decline from 1.7 million in 2014 to 0.5 million in 2023.

- Section 105 would restrict categorical eligibility, a current policy that allows states to determine eligibility for SNAP based on receipt of benefits in other programs for low-income people. CBO estimates that, on average, 1.8 million people with lower-than-average benefits would lose eligibility for the program if this provision were enacted. The number of people losing benefits would decline from 2.1 million in 2014 to 1.5 million in 2023."[28]

Sometimes a single point estimate of your best guess about the degree of magnitude will suffice. But in most cases, you should provide a range.

Trends Might Be the Basis of Projections

Projecting outcomes is about the future, but this does not mean that one can never glean useful information from trend data. Past trends will only provide a reasonable basis for making projections, however, if the implicit assumption holds that whatever factors influenced changes in outcomes in the past will continue to operate the same way going forward. For example, if the analyst seeks to use past trends in local public school district expenditures as the basis for a projection of how much the school district will spend over the next decade, she would need to determine if changes in student enrollment, among many other factors, will have approximately the same influence on district spending levels in the future as they did previously. But not all trends are stable. Maybe, to continue with this example, per-student education costs have been changing due to student demography, a shifting mix of state and federal education mandates, and other reasons so that an X percent increase in the student enrollment level may not result in a Y percent increase in district expenditures that was previously associated with an enrollment increment of the same size. Data series can also be subject to seasonal (e.g., traffic congestion levels) or cyclical (e.g., economic fluctuations associated with the business cycle, such as unemployment trends) trends, which also need to be taken into account.

Break-Even Estimates Can Shrink Uncertainty

"You have no evidence this will work," carp your critics. You—quite correctly—respond, "You have no evidence it won't." You are both right, because "evidence" about events that have not yet occurred is a contradiction in terms. Nevertheless, your critics make the valid point that you probably can't be very certain that your recommended policy option will work and that the *burden of justification* (not, of course, a burden of literal "proof") falls on you.[29] You will want to take up this burden using whatever strategic leverage you can muster.

This means that you will set the bar of justification as low as is reasonable. Typically, you will want to claim only that the recommended course of action is "sufficiently likely" to produce results that are good enough to justify the known costs and risks. This approach is known as "break-even" or "threshold" analysis. It is an astonishingly powerful—yet simple, intuitive, and commonsensical— conceptual lens. It builds a decision framework out of what is known or reasonably assumed and handles the residual uncertainties by comparing them to elements in this more secure frame.

Suppose, for instance, that some youth-guidance-oriented policy meant to reduce incarceration of juveniles is under consideration and has known costs of $1 million, but the level of effectiveness is speculative. You build a decision frame out of (1) a decision rule that says, "If the benefits exceed the costs, do it," and (2) a known fact about the costs, $1 million. You then evaluate the remaining uncertainty in these four steps:

1.   Locate the point of minimum acceptable effectiveness given the costs. Ask: "What is the minimum level of effectiveness this policy would have to achieve in order to justify our spending $1 million?" Your answer: "Different observers have different opinions about how much avoiding an incarceration is worth, but leaving that aside and going with my own values, I'd say that

a 15 percent reduction is the minimum I would accept given the expenditure of $1 million."[30]

2.   Referring back to your model of the processes that create the problem and hold it in place, ask: "What new processes, or changes in old ones, could conceivably produce this level of effectiveness?" This is largely a qualitative analysis. The answer might be this: "Based on previous documentation of how the guidance process works, we can safely say that it works in different ways with different sorts of kids—when it works at all, that is. It can provide about half the kids more constructive life choices; in about a quarter of the cases, it works through heightening the (realistic) perception of punishment; and in about a quarter of the cases, we are just crossing our fingers."

3.   Assess how likely (or unlikely) it is that the processes for improvement thus identified will actually produce the required—that is, the break-even—level of effectiveness. It is particularly helpful to ask whether the break-even level (15 percent, in this case) looks like a plausible number given what is known or assumed about the effectiveness in similar circumstances of similar sorts of interventions. If the number is implausibly high, you might then go on to ask whether special circumstances of some sort might be at work in this case to help achieve it. Note that in this and the previous step you must rely on what we might think of as "theory," or self-conscious and evidence-based reasoning about the way causal processes work. Typically, these are the weakest links in the chain of policy-analytic reasoning. That is why it is particularly important—and particularly difficult—to take this step as thoughtfully, self-critically, and responsibly as possible.

4.   Estimate the probability of failure and the political and other costs of having to accept failure—asking yourself whether these costs would be tolerable should they be incurred.

The federal government frequently uses break-even analysis to assess the merits of proposed regulations. For example, the federal government considered whether to issue a regulation designed to reduce the incidence of prison rape. The annual cost of implementation of the regulation was estimated at $470 million. The agency was not able to project the number of prison rapes the regulation would prevent. In addition, it had difficulty monetizing the cost of prison rapes to both victims and society. Under break-even analysis, however, the agency decided to go forward with the regulation. It found that at least 160,000 prison rapes occur each year, and it concluded that if a single rape prevention is valued at $500,000, the rule would be justified if it prevented only 1,600 rapes, or 1 percent of the total. The agency was confident that the new rule would achieve at least this minimum level of effectiveness.[31]

In the hope that it may be helpful to encourage readers to use break-even analysis (when appropriate, of course), we offer two more examples:

- Policy X for establishing a chain of wildlife refuges looks like an excellent choice to implement a broader conservation agenda, provided that the funding comes through as planned. But it might not, because federal grant-in-aid resources may not be forthcoming, or the governor may give the policy lower priority than she now promises, or some development interests that have their eye on two of the designated sites may find a way to block it. You interview your client, a state environmental agency director, and determine that she likes the program so much that she is willing to go for it if it has at least a fifty-fifty chance of working out. Your analysis can then focus her attention on why, after considerable research, you have concluded that it has a somewhat better (or somewhat worse) chance than fifty-fifty, even though you may find it impossible to specify exactly how much better (or worse).

- Building a new stadium for the Hometown Heroes looks like a good idea, given the nature of the costs and benefits, if average daily attendance turns out to be no fewer than ten thousand. That's the break-even attendance figure for you and the relevant decision-makers. It's up to them to decide, first, how confident they are that this break-even level will be reached and, then, whether that degree of confidence is enough to warrant making an affirmative decision. You can thus organize your presentation of facts and opinions to focus on these two key issues.[32]

Semantic Tip Assuming for the moment that benefits are uncertain while costs are not, ask yourself these two questions: (1) "Given what I know for sure about the costs of this alternative, what is the minimum help we need to get from Condition X to ensure adequately offsetting benefits?" and (2) "How reasonable is it to believe that Condition X will actually produce that minimum?"

See Box I-6 for an excerpt from a policy analysis report that confronts uncertainty.

Try Sensitivity Analysis

Which uncertainties are the most important, in the sense that relatively small changes in what you believe would cause you to change your mind about how desirable some alternative might be? By a process known as sensitivity analysis, you can discover these most important uncertainties. The procedures are somewhat technical (Morgan and Henrion 1990, chap. 8), but the intuition behind them is simple. Consider the several assumptions you have made on the way to your conclusion and suppose that each of them is somewhat mistaken.

Box I-6 An Illustrative Discussion of Confronting Uncertainty from a Policy Analysis Report

From: Deborah Gordon et al., *Know Your Oil: Creating a Global Oil-Climate Index* (Policy Brief), Carnegie Endowment for International Peace, 2015, 19–20, https://carnegieendowment.org/files/know_your_oil.pdf

OPGEE Challenges

The largest source of uncertainty in OPGEE [Oil Production Greenhouse Gas Emissions Estimator] is the lack of information on global oil fields. Many operators and many regions of the world have few formal data publication requirements. Data quality is also an ongoing issue in modeling upstream emissions. . . .

OPGEE utilizes about 50 data inputs, from simple entries like the name of the country where an oil field is located to challenging-to-obtain information such as an oil field's productivity index (expressed in daily production per unit pressure). Substantial research is involved in gathering OPGEE modeling data, which can be obtained from agencies, reports, scientific literature, and industry references.

OPGEE can function with limited data. The model has a comprehensive set of defaults and smart defaults that can fill in missing data. The more data found for a particular field, the more specific and less generic the emissions estimate becomes. All data are used to determine smarter default values over time.

As with all life-cycle assessment (LCA) models, boundaries must be drawn around the analysis. The handling of co-products that cross boundaries along the oil supply chain, from extraction to refining to end use, presents methodological challenges. For example, resulting GHG [greenhouse gas] emissions from condensates of light liquids, like ethane, that can be stripped off and sold before oil is transported to a refinery are not expressly included in OPGEE. Emissions associated with exploration occur at the beginning of an oil field development project and are spread over the life of the field. Extraction emissions that occur routinely are estimated at a point in time and assumed to recur over the lifetime of the oil field.

OPGEE treats liquid petroleum as the principal product of upstream processes. Emissions associated with electricity generated on-site or natural gas produced that is gathered, sold, and not flared is credited back or deducted from total emissions in OPGEE accounting. Any emissions from co-products like petcoke that are associated with upgrading heavy oils upstream of the refinery—as can be the case with Canadian bitumen and Venezuelan heavy oils—are not included in OPGEE unless the production process directly consumes petcoke (as in some oil-sands-based integrated mining and upgrading operations). Emissions from net production of petcoke have been included in the OPEM [Oil Products Emissions Module] downstream combustion module.

Recent studies have found that uncertainty in OPGEE's results is reduced after learning three to four key pieces of data about an oil field. After learning the ten most important pieces of information about an oil field, there is typically little benefit to learning the remaining data.

Imprecise data reporting introduces additional uncertainty. Errors in applying the model can lead to further uncertainty.

The key variables to enhance model precision include: steam-to-oil and water-to-oil ratios, flaring rates, and crude density (measured as API [American Petroleum Institute] gravity). Less important variables in the OPGEE model's ability to analyze GHG emissions include gas-to-oil ratios, oil production rates, and depth (except in extreme cases).

[Endnotes, figures and references to figures, and appendix omitted from excerpt.]

Now ask yourself this: "How big a mistake can I afford in this assumption before this analysis is in really big trouble?" The smaller the affordable mistake, the more sensitive is your analysis to the particular assumption.

It is not hard to examine these assumptions one at a time. But what if they pile up in such a way that you are "somewhat" wrong on two or three or four assumptions all at once? This situation is typically dealt with by a technique called "Monte Carlo simulation," which begins by recognizing that each assumption is in itself probabilistic and then combines the probabilities behind the assumptions to create a new set of probabilities about how the combination of assumptions will turn out. You can then say something like this: "Given the many possible scenarios that might occur, there is an 82 percent chance that the actual scenario would exceed our break-even requirement."[33]

But suppose that projections must be made for a future beset by multiple uncertainties, like climate change or the global configuration of military forces and technologies twenty-five years off, for which probability distributions are not known or are controversial. One promising approach makes use of any of an emerging set of computer-assisted projection techniques, generally known as long-term policy analysis. This approach is similar to Monte Carlo simulation in that it starts with scenarios about alternative futures, but instead it searches for policy choices that would be "robust," in the sense that they would not necessarily be the best but would satisfy the whole, or nearly the whole, array of minimum policy desiderata. The objective is to minimize the maximum "regret" that relevant parties might experience.[34]

Confront the Optimism Problem

Great ventures require optimism. Because even small ventures by government can affect so many lives, they are in their own way great. Hence, some realistic optimism is beneficial. But how do you guard against *excessive* optimism?

Scenario Writing. What scenarios might cause the proposal to fail to produce the desired outcome—that is, solving or sufficiently mitigating the policy problems? Do not create such scenarios from whole cloth; be realistic. And yet, let your imagination run a little so that you have a good chance of thinking of the most dangerous possibilities. In particular, think about the dangers of the implementation process, political and otherwise. Scenario writing also benefits from thinking about possible failures from a vantage point in the future looking backward. Consider the following scenarios:

- In a health or safety regulatory program, the scientific or technical knowledge necessary to produce rational and legally defensible standards may prove to be lacking. As a result, five years from now, symbolic politics, corruption, industry capture, or excessive regulatory zeal will have filled the vacuum.

- Time passes, and budgetary resources and political support that were once available slip away under the impact of electoral change and shifts in the economy. A terrorist-identification program, begun under nurturant leaders and accompanied by editorialists' applause, will have become consolidated with another program then taken over by a different bureaucratic unit and eventually will have disappeared.

- A successful state program designed to furnish technical assistance to extremely poor rural counties will have added a mandate to aid many not-so-poor urban counties, with the result that scarce program resources will have been dissipated and squandered. (We call this scenario "piling on"; see Bardach 1977.)

- A program that subsidizes research and development of "fish protein concentrate," intended as a cheap and nutritious food additive, is launched with great fanfare. Five years from now, it will have been stalled, permanently, by the US Food and Drug Administration, which will not have been able to assimilate this product into its standard operating procedures for regulatory review.

Semantic Tip Notice that these scenarios are written in the future perfect tense. Use of this verb tense encourages concreteness, which is a helpful stimulant to the imagination (Weick 1979, 195–200). It often helps your scenario writing to start with a list of adverse implementation outcomes, conjuring up one or more scenarios about how each of them might occur. Remember the list of such outcomes embodied in the scenarios just described: long delays, "capture" of program or policy benefits by a relatively undeserving and unintended constituency, excessive budgetary or administrative costs, scandal arising from fraud and waste, and administrative complexities that leave citizens (and program managers) uncertain as to what benefits are available or what regulations must be complied with.

Semantic Tip *Undesirable side effects.* Analysts are often cautioned to think about "unanticipated consequences." But this term is not appropriate, for it is often used to refer to perfectly anticipatable, though undesirable, side effects. Here are some common undesirable but foreseeable side effects in public programs:

- *Moral hazard* increases. That is, your policy has the effect of insulating people from the consequences of their actions. For example, increasing the size of unemployment benefits has the side effect of blunting the incentives to search for a replacement job.

- Reasonable regulation drifts toward *overregulation*, especially if the costs of overregulation are not perceptible to those who bear them. One possible adverse result of setting health or safety standards "too high" and enforcing them "too uniformly" is that you increase private-sector costs beyond some optimal level. For instance, given most people's preferences for safety, imposing auto bumper standards that cost some $25 per vehicle but have only trivial effects on improving vehicle crashworthiness would not pass a conventional benefit–cost test.
A second adverse result of overregulation might be that you inadvertently cause a shift away from the regulated activity into some other activity that—perversely—is less safe, less healthful, or more harmful. For instance, some observers argue that overregulating the safety features of nuclear power production has caused a shift toward coal, which they argue is much more hazardous than nuclear power.

- *Rent-seekers*—that is, interests looking out for profitable niches protected from full competition—distort the program to serve their own interests. It is not inevitable that suppliers of goods and services to the government, including civil servants, will find ways to capture "rents," but it often happens (e.g., with many defense contractors). Rent-seeking also occurs in less obvious ways—as when some regulated firms successfully lobby for regulations that impose much higher compliance costs on their competitors than on themselves.

- *The outcomes produced by one part of a complex policy design undermine the performance of another.* Policies sometimes contain multiple parts, such as both expenditure (or regulatory) and revenue-generation components. Undesirable consequences can arise when one part of the design produces outcomes that counteract the performance of another. For example, an education program paid for by earmarked revenues from a "sin" tax on cigarettes could lead to funding shortfalls for schools if the tax causes many smokers to quit. The same dynamic can occur if a regulatory inspectorate is financed by fines on violators. As the regulations take hold, fewer violations will occur, and the revenue to pay for inspections will dry up. To avoid this problem, analysts should seek to design policies whose constituent parts produce mutually reinforcing outcomes.

The ethical costs of optimism. It is hard to overstate the importance of worrying about the possible adverse side effects of otherwise "good" policies, not to mention the possibility that even intended main benefits may fail to materialize under many circumstances (see the chapter on "assessing your ignorance" in Behn and Vaupel 1982). The ethical policy analyst always poses the question, "If people actually were to follow my advice, what might be the costs of my having been wrong, and who would have to bear them?" Keep in mind that the analyst typically is *not* one of the parties who have to bear the costs of her mistakes.

To minimize the risk of undesirable side effects, take into account the incentives of the "targets" of behavioral change. A fundamental reason why a "solution" to a troubling situation may generate adverse consequences is that the analyst has failed to think about the incentives of the actors whose behavior a policy intervention is meant to alter. The point is not necessarily to condone the goals of such actors but rather to understand what really drives their behavior—so that a more effective, incentive-compatible intervention can be fashioned.

Consider "Ban the Box," a well-intended policy to prevent employers from inquiring about a person's criminal record in an initial job application. (Employers would still be allowed to ask about criminal records later in the hiring process.) The policy's aim is to give people with a criminal record a greater chance to interview for jobs and demonstrate their skills and qualifications before final hiring decisions are made. Advocates hope that "Ban the Box" will boost the low employment rate among ex-offenders, lessen racial disparities in employment, and reduce recidivism.

Unfortunately, rigorous studies have discovered that "Ban the Box" has the undesirable effect of reducing employment opportunities for young, low-skilled black men *without* criminal convictions.[35] What explains this outcome? Employers want to hire reliable, productive workers. Many have a preference against hiring people with criminal records because ex-offenders are more likely than non-offenders to have a history of violence or other antisocial behavior. If employers are prevented from knowing which applicants have a criminal record, they may respond by not interviewing young, low-skilled black men—the group most likely to have recent convictions.[36] In other words, employers engage in what economists call "statistical discrimination"—that is, they make assumptions about individuals based on averages among a group. To be sure, "Ban the Box" does not prevent employers from rejecting applicants with criminal records during the later stages of the hiring process. But screening and interviewing individual candidates is time-consuming, so busy employers may just avoid entire demographic groups altogether.

One plausible response to this adaptation by employers is to rely on civil rights laws banning racial discrimination in employment. However, such laws are difficult to enforce, especially with respect to discrimination that occurs early in the applicant review process.

An alternative approach to promoting the goal of increasing employment among ex-offenders (and reducing racial disparities in hiring) would take into account the desire of employers to have information about the productivity of applicants. The employers' desire for information could be satisfied by allowing individuals with criminal records to obtain "employability certificates" from courts.[37] Such certificates (which could be based on a judge's review of an ex-offender's completion of a training program) could help convince employers that an applicant with a criminal record has been rehabilitated and is "work-ready."

The "Ban the Box" case offers several broader lessons for policy analysis and design. First, adaptation is a general phenomenon and a frequent source of failure and backfire. A key challenge is thinking about how actors will respond to changes in the policy environment. It is often a good idea to consider within the menu of policy options alternatives that work with rather than against the incentives of policy targets.[38] Second, seemingly small changes (such as changing the timing of when an employer can learn about a job candidate's criminal record during the hiring process) can affect big movements in a system. Finally, information flows are of critical importance. The quantity and quality of information available to actors influences the level of uncertainty and thus how actors respond to policy measures and pursue their objectives.

The Emergent-Features Problem

Policy often intervenes in systems of some complexity, systems populated by actors who adapt to your interventions in surprising ways and whose adaptations lead other actors to create still further adaptations. Surprising behavior may emerge from such dynamics. How can you take such possibilities into account when you make your projections?

In many cases, you cannot, for the systems are too complex and too little understood. The macro-economy is an extreme case—the hypothetical responses of producer interests to "supply-side" tax cuts are a major source of contention between those who think the taxes generated by a growing economy will substantially offset the direct effects of the cuts and those who are deeply skeptical of this scenario. Few cases are that extreme, however, and you might make some progress with what might be called "the other-guy's-shoes" heuristic.

Imagine yourself in the other guy's shoes. Say to yourself, "If I were X, how would I act?" And then proceed to crawl into X's mind and play out, in your own mind, what X might do. Do this systematically for each of the important stakeholders or other affected parties. The value of this exercise is that you will discover them to be adapting in surprising ways to the new policy situation you may be creating.

For example, under chemical right-to-know laws, workers must be told what substances they have been exposed to, and they may examine health records maintained by employers. If you were a worker, how might you use this law? Might you use the information to quit your present job? To demand a higher wage or more protective equipment? To sue your employer or put pressure on your union representative?

And how would your union representative react to such pressure? Might this pressure make the representative's job harder—or perhaps easier in some way?

Now, suppose that you were an employer. Given what you expect your workers to do, you would face incentives to make adaptations or countermoves. Might you stop keeping all health records not explicitly required by law? Or continue keeping records but permit doctors to perform only selected lab tests? And if you were a worker and saw your employer doing these things, what countermoves would you make?

Not all the moves and countermoves of players wearing the other guy's shoes will necessarily lead to trouble for the policy alternative you are evaluating. Many such adaptation sequences may prove to be helpful, in the sense that they may help society to adjust to the changes set in motion by the new policy. At some point in the 1970s, the Federal Trade Commission (FTC) attacked the problem of retailers evading implied warranty obligations for defective products by selling installment debts to banks and other collectors that had no duty, under the so-called holder-in-due-course doctrine, to fix the product or to refrain from collecting on the installment debt. The FTC solution was, in effect, to abolish the protections of the holder-in-due-course doctrine. Banks complained that they did not want to go into the toaster repair business. But if you put yourself in the shoes of a bank manager suddenly obliged to become a toaster repairer, might you not have thought of contracting out your repair obligations to repair specialists, or perhaps arranging not to buy installment debts from retailers who you believed could not be relied upon to make good on their implied warranties?

Construct an Outcomes Matrix

The step of projecting outcomes leads you into a dense thicket of information. At some point along the way, you will probably need to stand back and assess complex and uncertain scenarios for perhaps two to five basic alternatives, combined with their principal variants. A convenient way to get an overview of all this information is to display it in an *outcomes matrix*. The typical outcomes matrix format arrays your policy alternatives down the rows and your evaluative criteria across the columns. Each cell contains the projected outcome of the row alternative as assessed by reference to the column criterion.

Table I-2 (p. 53) is an example. It appeared in a report by four Berkeley students in 2008 that had been requested by the international environmental group ICLEI–Local Governments for Sustainability.[39] They projected outcomes for eight alternatives ("scenarios," in their usage) across five criteria (in three clusters).[40] We do not vouch for the accuracy of their projections, though they tried the best they could to synthesize the diverse and sometimes contradictory research literature as it existed at the time. Of greater interest is their attempt to fill in the cells in a canonical matrix form. The alternatives are listed down the rows and the criteria across the columns. Three criteria are lumped together under the heading "Viability," though if space had permitted, the students might have made a separate column for each. The analysis applies to a representative US city called Anytown. Note that the matrix is labeled as a "comparative analysis." Each projection is compared to a baseline projection for the year 2050, showing only the difference between the baseline projection and the estimated projection for the indicated alternative. Most cells contain a projected range rather than a single point estimate. In Step Six, we come back to Table I-2 and discuss how this comparative setup facilitates confronting the trade-offs.

An outcomes matrix at this stage of your work is a scratch-pad affair, useful for you and your team members and perhaps a friendly outsider or two. Its main function is to help you see what you have in hand and what you still need to learn about. A secondary function is to prepare to confront the trade-offs (see Step Six). If the matrix looks to you large and complicated, you may be encouraged to shrink it: conceptualize some alternatives as mere variants of more or less the same thing, get rid of alternatives that are obvious losers, and omit criteria that don't differentiate among alternatives (i.e., all the alternatives appear to do about as well or as poorly with respect to these criteria). The students who produced Table I-2 excluded three alternatives that they had originally considered: a local cap-and-trade program, leveraging collective purchasing power in energy markets, and urban forestry.

You may find it useful to go through this exercise more than once, as your analysis evolves over time. (Table I-2 is the final version of several matrices that the student group made.)

A later version of such a matrix may also prove useful when you tell your story (see Step Eight). However, unless the matrix is very well designed and explained, it can impede the flow of your story rather than assist it.

Semantic Tip   Here is a tip with a graphic dimension. Take advantage of the fact that being listed earlier (more leftward) in the matrix is usually taken to signify greater importance. Even if you are unsure how to weight criteria on some cardinal scale, with equal intervals assumed between all points, you might feel better about an ordinal scale, requiring judgments only of more than and less than. Put what you think should be the weightier criteria in the more leftward columns. A common error that occurs in labeling the criteria columns in such a matrix is to fail to indicate what value is at stake and in what dimensions the measurement is being done. For instance, if you are assessing a rental subsidy program and you enter a plus sign in a column labeled "Landlord/Tenant Relations," the reader may not know whether you think relations will become more harmonious, more confrontational, less dominated by landlords, less dominated by tenants, or something else. It is not sufficient that your surrounding text makes your intention clear; the matrix label itself must be informative. In many cases, it helps to insert the term *maximize* or *minimize* in the criterion label. Table I-2 is exemplary in almost all respects, except that the column labels do not include such words. It happens that the meaning is quite clear from the context, of course, but in the interests of "analytic hygiene" it would have been better to include them.

If you cannot fill in the cell with a quantitatively expressed description of the projected outcome, you may have to settle for a verbal descriptor such as "very good" or a symbolic descriptor such as + or −. The operative word here, though, is *cannot*. Quantification goes a long way toward making an analysis useful, and rough yet adequate quantification is easier than you might suppose. Remember, also, the heuristic of increasing or decreasing "the odds," mentioned in "Step One: Define the Problem."

In listing or stating criteria, speak in the declarative, not the interrogative. "How equitable is the final budget outcome?" is not a criterion; it is a question. "Maximize equity" is a criterion.

But Policy Contexts Differ

Suppose the policy in question applies to heterogeneous policy contexts, such as different states or different counties within a state or different neighborhoods within a city. Suppose, further, that we should expect policy context to matter. Perhaps the policy would be suited to a well-off urbanized state but not to a low-wealth rural state or to a state with a strong populist tradition. Although the authors of the greenhouse gas study above may have been justified in using a hypothetical average "Anytown" as their base case, this is not always sensible. Demographic and other differences in context may imply that, while Anytown represents the broad mainstream well enough, "outlier" cases exist that could fare very differently.

One way to handle this is to break the analysis into as many different chunks as you need to handle the variety of important policy contexts. This should help you conceptualize variants that "tweak" a basic policy strategy so as to fit better the variety of contexts in which it will have to work. A citywide policy to encourage fire-resistant roofing materials on new and replacement roofs, for instance, could also incorporate loan assistance to building owners differentially targeted to high-risk areas and/or to higher- and lower-income property owners.

But what is a "policy context" anyway? "Context" does not have a stable, nicely circumscribed meaning. Just about anything that isn't "the alternative being considered" can be called "context." Income, race, residential density, and other such demographic features are often taken to be important to policy context. But this is not always true. And sometimes features that are not "obvious" or commonsensical are indeed important, like the degree of prior experience a community has had absorbing new immigrants or implementing novel central-government initiatives. In an abstract sense, policy-relevant context features are those that you cannot control but that probably make a difference to the eventual worth of the chosen policy.

The features of a relevant context are sometimes numerous and interconnected, so much so that one wants to handle them as a stylized bundle. For example, a fairly large jurisdiction, like an American state, often contains a number of smaller jurisdictions to which a statewide policy is applied. It would be unwieldy and unhelpful to analyze the context of each of the hundreds or thousands of localities with a given state separately. If, however, you can divide the whole field on which policy is to be applied into just a few such bundles, you can do subanalyses of three or four of them and feel some confidence that you have a sample that, if not "representative," nevertheless captures the mainstream and the principal outliers.

So how do we fit this into an analysis done for a statewide policy in a state with many different-size cities? The first task is to reduce the number of contexts to something manageable. Three is a nice number. The second is to create abstractions—"ideal types" in social science jargon—that effectively stand in for real places. The ideal types can even be given names for easy reference—for instance, "Gotham" for very large cities, "Middletown" for medium-sized cities, and "Fernville" for small localities. Each of these ideal types can be attached to the problem definition. At this point, doing so expands the number of problems from one to three. We are creating a "separate problem" for each ideal-type-characterized context.

Setup for the Next Step

A useful test of whether the projecting outcomes step has been done well is that the outcomes should be characterized in such a way that is easy for the analyst (or anyone) to calibrate the trade-offs. (Calibration, of course, is not the only process involved in confronting trade-offs, as will be discussed in the coming section; values matter too.)

Begin by making a table like Table I-3, which concerns a policy problem faced by a municipal library system in reaching out to the poorer, and

TABLE I-3

Outreach to Poorer Areas by Municipal Library

Alternatives/ outcomes	Books borrowed in outreach areas (per year)	Borrowers in outreach areas (per year)	Annual cost ($ per year)	Net political payoff to council member Y*
Base case: continue present trends	60,000	15,000	2,000,000	0
Bookmobile biweekly each area	80,000	20,000	2,500,000	200; 150
Bookmobile once weekly only the poorer areas	75,000	18,000	2,350,000	100; 50
Book fairs twice yearly in 25 public schools	85,000	21,000	2,100,000	0; 0

*Additional votes in next two elections minus votes lost.

less inclined toward reading, areas of the city. This table projects the whole outcome, with respect to each of the important criteria, of each alternative under consideration, including (of course) "Let present trends continue." It provides the big picture of what is at stake in the world for the choices at hand.

Box I-7 displays a specimen from the outcomes projection section of a policy analysis report. Note the use of a base case, the acknowledgment of data limitations, and that the anticipated increases in primary care physicians are discussed in terms of the amount per hundred-thousand population to facilitate comparisons of projected outcomes across alternatives.

STEP SIX: CONFRONT THE TRADE-OFFS

It sometimes happens that one of the policy alternatives under consideration is expected to produce a better outcome than any of the other alternatives with regard to every single evaluative criterion. In that case—called "dominance"—there are no trade-offs among the alternatives.[41] Usually, though, you are less fortunate, and you must clarify the trade-offs between outcomes associated with different policy options for the sake of your client or audience.[42]

Focus on Outcomes

A common pitfall in confronting trade-offs is to think and speak of the trade-offs as being across *alternatives* rather than across projected *outcomes*—for example, "trading off twenty foot-patrol police officers in the late-night hours against a lower-maintenance-cost fleet of police vehicles." Although such a trade-off exists, with a second's thought you'll see that you can't do anything at all with it. Both alternatives must first be converted into outcomes before genuine trade-offs can be confronted. Thus, the competing outcomes might be fifty (plus or minus) burglaries per year prevented by the foot-patrol officers versus a savings of $300,000 in fleet maintenance.

The most common trade-off is between money and a good or service received by some proportion of the citizenry, such as extending library hours from 8 p.m. till 10 p.m., weighed against a cost of $200,000 annually. Another common trade-off, especially in regulatory policies, involves weighing privately borne costs (a company's installing pollution abatement equipment) against social benefits (improved health of the affected population and the protection of forests). If the projected outcomes can be monetized—that is, expressed in dollar terms—it is sometimes simple to evaluate the trade-offs. Just choose the option that yields the largest net value, once costs have been subtracted from benefits. This procedure applies nicely if budgets, and therefore the scope of the

Box I-7 An Illustrative Example of "Project the Outcomes" from a Policy Analysis Report

From: Mark W. Friedberg et al., *Evaluation of Policy Options for Increasing the Availability of Primary Care Services in Rural Washington State,* **RAND Corporation, 2016, xii–xiv, https://www.rand .org/pubs/research_reports/RR1620.html**

Base-Case Projections of the Rural and Urban Primary Care Workforce

Our predictive models estimated declines in the number of primary care physicians per 100,000 population in both rural and urban areas from 2013 to 2025: 3.66 fewer primary care physicians per 100,000 population in rural counties by 2025, 4.14 fewer in urban counties, 5.07 fewer outside Seattle, and 3.22 fewer within Seattle. These estimated declines were driven largely by recent increases in the percentage of primary care physicians ages 55 and older, many of whom are likely to retire by 2025. In contrast, we projected increases from 2013 to 2025 of 5.38 to 7.79 nurse practitioners (NPs) and 1.84 to 3.08 physician assistants (PAs) per 100,000 population in Washington State. . . .

Open the Elson S. Floyd College of Medicine at Washington State University [WSU]

We estimated that opening the new medical school in 2017, beginning with 60 students and reaching a steady-state enrollment of 320 students in 2022, would be associated with increases in 2025 of 0.39 primary care physicians per 100,000 population in rural Washington counties, 0.59 in urban counties, 0.76 in Seattle, and 0.39 in Washington counties outside Seattle. These estimated effects of the new medical school offset approximately 11 percent of the projected decrease in rural per capita primary care physician supply by 2025, 14 percent of the projected decrease in urban counties, 12 percent of the projected decrease within Seattle, and 15 percent of the projected decrease outside Seattle.

Increase the Number of Primary Care Residency Positions in Washington State

We modeled residency policy options ranging up to a 100-percent expansion (i.e., a doubling of primary care residency sizes outside Seattle). The estimated effects of 100-percent primary care residency expansion (adding 36 primary care residents) were larger than the estimated effects of opening the new medical school at WSU, without residency program expansion. However, none of the modeled residency scenarios had an estimated effect sufficient to offset the predicted decline in the number of rural primary care physicians (or primary care physicians outside Seattle) per 100,000 population. For the 100-percent residency size expansions, estimated effects ranged from 1.11 primary care physicians per 100,000 population (27 percent of the projected decrease) in urban counties to 2.00 primary care physicians per 100,000 population (55 percent of the projected decrease) in rural counties by 2025.

Increase the Availability of Educational Loan-Repayment Incentives

To estimate the effect of expanding state-funded loan-repayment incentives in rural areas, we analyzed relationships between the number of National Health Service Corps (NHSC) primary care positions and primary care supply in rural counties. We found that, for each new primary care NHSC position opened per 100,000 county population, the estimated increase was 0.24 primary care physicians per 100,000 county population. Therefore, we estimated that doubling the number of primary care NHSC positions in rural Washington State (by adding 30 more such positions to rural counties, with approximate cumulative population 700,000) would produce an increase of 1.03 primary care physicians per 100,000 population.

Improve the Quality of High School Education in Rural Washington State

Because we lacked longitudinal data on high school quality (measured as proficiency rates on standardized tests of mathematics and of reading and language arts), we fit cross-sectional models that estimated the effect of increasing proficiency rates on these standardized tests by 0.2 standard deviations among high schools in rural Washington counties. We estimated that this improvement in high school quality would be associated with an increase of 0.80 primary care physicians per 100,000 population in rural Washington, or approximately 22 percent of the projected decline in per capita rural primary care physicians expected by 2025. However, because these models were cross-sectional and the time required to improve school performance is unclear, we cannot estimate the number of years required to achieve this estimated effect.

[The report also projected outcomes from several other alternatives, including preserving rural hospitals in Washington State and increasing Medicaid payment rates for primary care physicians in rural Washington State, among others; references to tables omitted from excerpt.]

Source: Mark W. Friedberg et al., *Evaluation of Policy Options for Increasing the Availability of Primary Care Services in Rural Washington State*, RAND Corporation, 2016.

activity, are not limited. But it can run afoul of another monetary consideration, cost-effectiveness per unit of activity, if budgets or other inputs are limited. In Table I-2 (p. 53), note that the high-density residential development option—presumably limited in extent because of the limited likely scope of new development—is more cost-effective than any other activity but is less efficacious than all the others, too.

In Table I-2, (p. 53) we see that there is no dominant outcome. The really efficacious options, involving a carbon tax, are not viable politically. Retrofitting existing buildings is apparently more efficacious than meeting green standards in new buildings, but it is a strategy deemed by the student-authors to be less viable than the latter. And, as we said earlier, making new developments denser, although cost-effective, is not very efficacious.

The student-authors did not recommend choosing among these alternatives, however, but recommended doing as many of them at one time as was feasible ("viable"). The trade-offs analysis would nonetheless permit decision-makers, and the public, to prioritize which alternatives to emphasize in the likely case that priorities needed to be set. In their view, setting standards for energy efficiency in buildings was the first order of business.

Establish Commensurability

Suppose some Alternative A_1 stacks up very well on Criterion C_1, moderately well on C_2, and poorly on C_3. And suppose that A_2 stacks up in the opposite way. We can choose between the two alternatives only if we can weight the importance of the criteria and if we can express their relative weights in units that are commensurable across the criteria. As you may have heard, money is everybody's favorite candidate for the commensurable metric. Using money as the metric is a very good idea, and it often works much better than you might imagine. For instance, even the "value" of life can sometimes be described reasonably well in the metric "willingness to pay X dollars for a reduction in the risk of death by Y percent a year," or something like it.

It is sometimes even possible, using money as a common metric, to compare apples and oranges, through the use of "willingness to pay" for hard-to-quantify outcomes like "better privacy protection" or "less-noisy motor scooters." This is the standard approach of benefit–cost analysis. How one does this is a very technical matter, and occasionally very controversial as well.[43]

In any case, a willingness-to-pay approach eventually runs into limits. To reach a summary judgment as to how much political equality to give up in a political redistricting case, for instance, in exchange for more African American voter power, it seems impossible even to state the trade-off in meaningful terms. In general, this problem is known as the "multiattribute problem." In some deep sense, the problem is logically insoluble, although some heuristics are available to help trim it down to its irreducible size.[44]

Break-Even Analysis Revisited. We have seen how break-even analysis can help you both to focus on which residual uncertainties you will have to estimate and to frame the terms in which those estimates must be given (e.g., "We have to believe Alternative A_1 will produce at least X results in order to justify choosing it"). We turn now to how break-even analysis can also help to solve commensurability problems.

Consider those policy areas, such as safety regulation, where we are often implicitly trading off dollars against risks to life. It might be supposed that in order to assess these proposals, you would have to decide what a human life is *really worth*—a task many of us, quite understandably, are unwilling to perform. The task is made somewhat more tractable, however, if you work with quantitative estimates and apply break-even analysis. Suppose, for instance, that you are considering whether or not to impose on the auto industry a new design standard that will improve safety and save an estimated twenty-five lives every year into the indefinite future. The cost of meeting the standard is estimated at $50 million per year indefinitely. The trade-off at the margin appears to be, therefore, "$2 million per life." But you don't have to answer the question, "What's a human life really worth?" in order to make at least some sense of this decision. You do have to answer the question, "Is a statistical life (that is, the life of an unknown individual 'drawn' in a random manner from some population, rather than a named person's life) worth at least $2 million?" That is a break-even analysis sort of question. For reasons best known to yourself, it may be obvious to you that a statistical life surely is—or isn't—worth that much. And although it's very difficult to decide whether the worth of a statistical life falls on one or the other side of some monetary boundary, it's a lot less difficult than coming up with a point value.

Even this sort of trade-off calculation is troubling to many people, and some find it morally repugnant. Unfortunately, repugnant or not, it is in a sense inevitable. Whatever position you take on the auto safety design standard described, you are by implication also taking a position on the dollars/risk-to-life trade-off: If you favor the standard, you implicitly believe the trade-off is worthwhile, whereas if you oppose it, you don't. Fortunately, this logical implication has its uses. You may in many circumstances quite sensibly prefer to rely on your intuition rather than on some complicated systematic method. Once you have reached your conclusion on that basis, though, you should check your intuition by asking yourself, "Since the implication of my policy choice is that I value X as being worth at least (or at most) thus-and-such, do I really believe that?"

Frame Trade-Offs Crisply. That is one semantic strategy for thinking about trade-offs. We encountered another one on page 38 in discussing the weighting of criteria. When choosing between two railroad routes, we asked how heavily the decision-maker wished to weight the welfare of ten households forced out of their homes versus saving $20 million on construction of the more accommodating route. We can now suggest another strategy for framing trade-offs crisply involving long division. It might help to think about the trade-off here in terms of an "average" individual family rather than the aggregate of ten households. Is it worth spending $2 million to avoid removing a single family from their home?

But magnitudes are important as well. And once you have projected outcomes, you are in a better position to bring them into the thinking about trade-offs too. In the railroad routing example, would it make sense to approach the trade-off challenge by doing some long division? It might be helpful to think about a single "average" homeowner instead of the ten and ask whether it's worth spending $2 million ("on average") to avoid imposing grief on this family. We should note, by the way, that, even though this is in one important respect a complex moral question, getting some numbers on the table is very helpful, even essential. Just as it is important to know the numbers twenty million, ten, and two million, we also need to remember the number three hundred thousand, the amount of compensation offered to offset at least some of the average family's distress. It is furthermore necessary to remember that we are dealing with averages here for analytical convenience only but that in the actual situation some families will experience distress much greater than the average and some much less.

Trade-Offs Are About Increments

The key to confronting trade-offs is to compare increments. "If we spend an extra X dollars for an extra unit of Service Y, we can get an extra Z units of good outcome." This kind of analysis puts the decision-maker in the position to answer the question, "Does society (or do you) value Z more or less than outcome X?" and then to follow the obvious implication of the answer: if yes, decide for another unit of Y; if no, don't.

The outcomes projections you have already done—the cells in your matrix—set you up to make these comparisons. All outcomes are expressed as increments or decrements with respect to some base case outcomes. From Table I-2 we learn that if we choose incentives for photovoltaic distribution (PV) over a policy of high-density residential development, we might expect about a 1.5 percent greater decrease in carbon emissions, but the cost per ton of those decreases will be higher by somewhere between $841 and $1,318. We also learn from Table I-2 that there are no trade-offs between the two policies in terms of the three "viability" dimensions, since they are rated the same on all.

The comparisons among increments are done essentially by subtraction. The values for high-density residential development have been subtracted from those for PV incentives. The residuals, following the subtraction, characterize the ways in which the two policies differ in their outcomes. One gets us more abatement, while the other is more cost-effective. These, of course, are only some of many trade-offs worth considering, others of which do not show up in Table I-2. Total cost, for instance, would probably be of interest, but one needs to go outside the table to get this information. Note what has dropped out of the discussion: the ways in which these two policies are similar—that is, accomplish the same goals. Presumably both are able to curb a substantial amount of carbon emissions, but this fact has disappeared from Table I-2 and therefore from the discussion of that table in this section. This is because Table I-2 has entered only information about how the alternatives considered improve upon (or fall short of) what would happen if the base case (called baseline by the student authors) were chosen. Is this disappearance helpful or not? It is not helpful if we want to be reminded of the overall stakes in the policy choice. But it is helpful if we want to focus, without distracting clutter, on the consequences of choice, which are the incremental differences between the outcomes projected from various alternatives.

Returning to our municipal library example, Table I-3 draws out what is at stake in the world for the alternatives under consideration. But it does not, by itself, help us to focus on the small pictures that show the incremental differences and, therefore, the trade-offs between the outcomes of the various alternatives.

To do that, Table I-4 needs to be created out of Table I-3. This can be done in the mind alone or, more reliably, with pencil and paper or on a spreadsheet program. Table I-4 focuses on the incremental differences between each of the alternatives and the base case. It focuses on how much the world would differ were we to choose a given alternative rather than to let the base case unfold. Essentially, it is created out of Table I-3 by subtracting the base case outcomes from the outcomes of each of the projected alternatives. The result tells you what you gain or lose on the several criterion dimensions by choosing a particular alternative over the base case.

But it does not tell you what you get by choosing one alternative over another alternative that is not the base case. In the example at hand, three such comparisons are possible. In a problem with, say, five alternatives other than the base case, the three become nine. One could make a separate table for each such comparison. But in most cases this would be wasteful. Instead, one could pick the most plausible comparison and discard the alternative that looks less good—and keep on doing this until one is confident that the best survives.

TABLE I-4

Incremental Comparisons between Each Alternative and the Base Case

Alternatives/ outcomes	Additional books borrowed in outreach areas (per year)	Additional borrowers in outreach areas (per year)	Annual cost ($ per year)	Net political payoff to council member Y*
Base case: continue present trends	0	0	0	0
Bookmobile biweekly each area	20,000	5,000	500,000	200; 150
Bookmobile once weekly only the poorer areas	15,000	3,000	350,000	100; 50
Book fairs twice yearly in 25 public schools	25,000	6,000	100,000	0; 0

*Additional votes in next two elections minus votes lost

This procedure would be suitable, however, if we were to believe that the analyst's choices along the way would be the same as those of the client. However, the analyst cannot be sure this is true. His duty to the client would be to present a few (three or four?) alternatives to the client with the pros and cons of each, and some suggestions as to where the client should look for some key trade-offs of likely interest.

Semantic Tip A linguistic device to help you stay focused on the margin is frequent use of the word *extra*. Note that this word appears three times in the example analysis in the first paragraph of this section.

Some units of Service Y can be purchased only in "lumps" larger than one—sometimes much larger. Consider transportation services provided by highways and bridges. T might be one passenger trip from A to B, but most transportation construction projects (highway enlargements, new bridge crossings) can be undertaken only for minimum bundles of T that run into the thousands of trips. Or suppose that a police chief must choose one of two "lumpy" alternatives such as $1 million per year for more overtime on the night shift or $250,000 per year for more rapid replacement of police cars. The first alternative is lumpy because the police union insists on a minimum overtime rate for all 150 officers on the shift, and the second is lumpy because the auto supplier charges much less per vehicle after some threshold number of vehicles. If, say, the projected decrease in burglaries from increased overtime is 200 per year and that from newer vehicles is 50, the trade-off confronting the decision-maker at the margin is an extra $5,000 per extra burglary prevented. In this case, the margin is a lumpy 150 burglaries and $750,000. (Criteria other than burglary prevention and cost efficiency would, of course, be relevant to this problem.)

The Better and the Worse

Trade-offs that are quantified are more useful than trade-offs that are not quantified. But quantification is frequently not possible. Suppose, for instance, that the board of a local community foundation wants advice about how to evaluate grant applications for a social services activity, and you envision these alternatives: invest more in getting to know the human capacities in the applicant organization, collect better data about supposed outcomes of the activity, and seek the advice of consultants who are expert in the activity in question. The three alternatives differ in their strengths and weaknesses. Hence there are trade-offs among them. Although it is hard or impossible to quantify these trade-offs, it is still possible to rank order the three alternatives. The trade-offs then become implicit rather than explicit. But that is better than not confronting them at all.

Rank-ordering is especially useful when you face an uncertain "budget" constraint. This budget can be in money or in personnel time or in expected administrative hassle or in political favors that need to be called in—practically anything, that is, that is important to policy execution and is in limited supply. The uncertainty is about what exactly the limits are. Does the board of the community foundation wish to allocate more money or more time, or more of each, to evaluating grant applications? The policy analyst does not know in advance, and probably the board does not know either. Rank-ordering of alternatives tells decision-makers, in effect, "Start with the ones at the top, and keep going down until you run out of whatever you think is the relevant budget."

STEP SEVEN: STOP, FOCUS, NARROW, DEEPEN, DECIDE!

Up to this point, progress on the Eightfold Path has mainly bred expansion: of problem elements, alternatives, and criteria. It may also have bred an undesirable formalism, such that lists of these items may have come to have a life of their own. The outcomes matrix, which ideally would have served as a sort of "rough draft with attitude," may have displaced the problem with which the project began. But the object of all your analytic effort should not be merely to present the client with a list of well-worked-out options. It should be to ensure that at least one of them—and more than one, if possible—would be an excellent choice to take aim at solving, or mitigating, the problem.

At a minimum, this need to focus, narrow, and deepen your analysis of the most promising alternative(s) means that you must think very seriously about (1) the politics of getting this alternative legitimated and adopted and (2) the design of the ongoing institutional features that will have the power and resources to implement the policy or program in the long run.[45]

At Step Seven, it is useful to remind yourself that the Eightfold Path is an *iterative* process. Before finalizing your analysis, pause, take stock, look at the big picture, review what you've done, and make any changes. The pitfalls of working through a problem are numerous, and even experienced policy analysts can get it wrong. Box I-8 presents a selective list of pitfalls for each step of the Eightfold Path (along with semantic remedies). These are some of the most common and treacherous pitfalls in our experience, but we invite you to add your own to this list—and let us know if you have better candidates for the next edition.

As another check on whether you have done your job well to this point, even though you personally may not be the decision-maker, you should now pretend that you are. Then, decide what to do, based on your own analysis. If you find this decision difficult or troublesome, the reason may be that you have not clarified the trade-offs sufficiently, or that you have not thought quite enough about the political barriers to adoption or probability of serious implementation problems emerging (or not emerging), or that a crucial cost estimate is still too fuzzy and uncertain, or that you have not approximated carefully enough the elasticity of some important demand curve, and so on.

Think of it this way: unless you can convince *yourself* of the plausibility of some course of action, you probably won't be able to convince your client—and rightly so.

Of course, when you tell your story to your client or any other audience, you may not think it appropriate to make reference to your own decision. You may choose, instead, to simply limit your story to a clarification of the relevant trade-offs and leave the decision completely up to the audience.

Box I-9 displays a portion of a report from the Legislative Analyst's Office (LAO) in California that encapsulates many of the key elements of this step. The excerpted section organizes and clarifies the good and the bad, the advantages and the disadvantages of the options, and also explains what alternatives are not recommended. Doing Step Seven well sets up the analyst to move easily to the final step, telling your story.

Box I-8 The Eightfold Path:
Pitfalls and Semantic Remedies

Define the Problem. Pitfall: unwittingly smuggling a solution into the problem definition. (Semantic) remedy: "Our problem is there is too little [too much] X." Or: "Our problem is that X is growing too fast [too slowly]."

Assemble Some Evidence. Pitfall: data for their own sake—that is, spending time collecting a lot of data without sufficient attention as to whether the data can be transformed into information and the information into evidence. Corollary pitfall: ending up without the evidence you really want. Remedy: "This is evidence for the important idea that . . ."

Construct the Alternatives. Pitfall: too vague specification of what the alternative really is. Not behavioral or concrete enough. Remedy: "If we do this, next Monday morning Josephine and Roger should . . ."

Select the Criteria. Pitfall: they apply to the outcome, not to the alternatives. Remedy: use "maximize" or "minimize" or "Do enough to . . ."

Project the Outcomes. Pitfall: ignoring uncertainty. Remedy: "The odds this will happen are . . ." Or: "Here is the likely range of possibilities, with the most likely being in the middle." (The latter framing is good if you want to rid yourself of thinking about low probabilities, as the odds of the whole range encompassing the outcomes would be very high, even if any particular outcome's odds would be low.)

Confront the Trade-Offs. Pitfall: not focusing on the margin. Remedy: "The gain of extra X is worth giving up extra Y."

Decide. Pitfall: shifting the burdens of your own vague analysis to the client or someone else. Remedy: "If I were making this decision by myself, here is exactly what I would do . . ."

Tell Your Story. Pitfall: vagueness caused by pulling punches, and using euphemisms and circumlocutions. Remedy: "We have this problem, and here is what I think we should do about it, though admittedly there are many challenges along the way . . ."

Box I-9 An Illustrative Example of "Stop, Focus, Narrow, Deepen, Decide!" from a Policy Analysis Report

From: *Analysis of the 2004–05 Budget Bill*, Legislative Analyst's Office, February 2004, https://lao.ca.gov/analysis_2004/health_ss/hss_12_4280_anl04.htm#_Toc64277937

Healthy Families Program

Background

Program Draws Down Federal Matching Funds. The federal *Balanced Budget Act of 1997* (BBA) made available approximately $40 billion in federal funds over ten years to states to expand health care coverage for children under the State Children's Health Insurance Program (SCHIP). The BBA also provided states with an enhanced federal match as a financial incentive to cover children in families with incomes above the previous limits of their Medicaid programs. Under SCHIP, the federal government provides states with flexibility in designing a program.

California decided in 1997 to use its approximately $4.5 billion share of SCHIP funding to implement the state's Healthy Families Program. Funding for the program generally is on a 2-to-1 federal/state matching basis. Families pay a relatively low monthly premium and can choose from a selection of managed care plans for their children. Coverage is similar to that offered to state employees and includes dental, vision, and basic mental health care benefits. The Healthy Families Program also covers more intensive mental health services for children with serious emotional disturbances, which are directly provided through county mental health systems and supported primarily with county and federal funding. . . .

Enrollment Cap Proposal Raises Policy Concerns

The Governor's budget proposal to cap Healthy Families Program enrollment, while feasible and effective in addressing the state's fiscal problems, raises a number of issues. We recommend against this approach because other alternatives are available to the Legislature to hold down the cost of the Healthy Families Program. . . .

Governor's Proposal Has Some Advantages

Savings Would Be Realized. The overall administration proposal to cap health and social services program caseloads is discussed generally in the

"Crosscutting Issues" section of this chapter. Policy issues of particular importance to the Healthy Families Program are discussed below.

Our analysis of the Governor's proposal indicates that it is technically feasible and would probably generate program savings of the magnitude estimated by the administration. Assuming the cap were maintained, the amount of savings achieved from a freeze on enrollment would grow significantly over time and contribute to addressing the state's structural imbalance between revenues and expenditures.

The administration's approach would also be less disruptive to the ongoing operation of the program than other possible approaches for achieving savings. No child now receiving coverage through the Healthy Families Program would lose his or her benefits. It is also possible that the prospect of long waiting lists would provide additional incentive for parents of Healthy Families children to become more diligent about submitting annual eligibility documents in a timely fashion, and reduce the high rate of disenrollment of children from the program.

Several Issues Warrant Consideration

The Governor's proposal to cap program enrollment in Healthy Families (as well as comparable caps on other health and social services programs) raises a number of significant policy issues that the Legislature may wish to consider.

Waiting Lists Could Create Inequities. The administration's proposal raises some distinct equity issues. First, children who entered the program before January 1, 2004 would be treated differently than children who applied after that date even though they met the same eligibility criteria. Also, the administration proposal is for a first-come, first-served approach in which the first person on a waiting list would be added to the Healthy Families Program caseload as children were disenrolled and "room" was created for additional children on program rolls. While this approach is equitable—all children on the waiting list would be treated alike—it also raises other questions of fairness, in that children would be added to program enrollment in the future regardless of a child's medical needs or family income level. . . .

Time on Waiting List May Be Underestimated. Another concern is that the waiting time for an applicant to actually receive health coverage could turn out to be longer than the maximum of six months estimated by the administration. That estimate is based on current disenrollment and enrollment trends. To the extent that parents' behavior changed, as discussed above, so that disenrollment rates in the program decreased,

(Continued)

(Continued)

the waiting period for coverage could be longer than projected. As noted earlier, the waiting period for enrollees would be likely to exceed one year by June 2006. . . .

State Would Lose Additional SCHIP Funds. The proposal to cap enrollment in the Healthy Families Program would result in state savings, but also reduce by about $55 million the amount of federal SCHIP funds being drawn down for health coverage of the uninsured. Since the inception of the Healthy Families Program, California has struggled to fully utilize its federal allotment of SCHIP funds. To date, the state has reverted $1.1 billion in unspent funds back to the federal government, which was redistributed to other states that were able to expend their allotment within the specified time period. As of May 2003, California had approximately $1.9 billion in unspent SCHIP funds remaining. We would acknowledge, however, that some other strategies for containing state costs for Healthy Families coverage would also add to the amount of SCHIP funds that would go unspent.

Some Children Would Lose Insurance Coverage. The Healthy Families Program was established to operate in tandem with Medi-Cal to ensure seamless health care coverage for children ages 0 to 19 living in families earning up to 250 percent of the FPL [federal poverty level]. Due to the income and age-based eligibility structure for both programs, the proposed enrollment cap would place certain children who were enrolled in Medi-Cal at risk of losing insurance coverage. Specifically, upon reaching their first and sixth birthday, children who would traditionally transition to the Healthy Families Program because their families' incomes would no longer qualify them for Medi-Cal would instead be placed on a waiting list for coverage.

Analyst's Recommendation

Other Alternatives Available . . . After weighing the advantages of imposing an enrollment cap on Healthy Families against the issues discussed above, we recommend against the Governor's proposal because, in our view, other alternatives are available to the Legislature to hold down the cost of the Healthy Families Program. As we will discuss later in this analysis, we believe there are other strategies that could be adopted to reduce program spending that would be more equitable to beneficiaries, more consistent with other state efforts to assist the uninsured, and that would make more effective use of the available federal SCHIP funds.

. . . But if Proposal Is Adopted. Should the Legislature decide to adopt the Governor's proposal, there are several steps it could take to address

some of the issues we have outlined. In that event, we would recommend that the Legislature consider the following actions:

- Modify the first-come, first-served approach to prioritize for Healthy Families coverage the poorest eligible children, and-or those with the most significant medical needs. These actions would partly reduce the savings but ensure that state funds are used for those who are most needy.

- Modify the CHIM [County Health Initiative Matching Fund] program to allow coverage of individuals otherwise eligible for Healthy Families but placed on a waiting list. This could address the inequity by which CHIM children in families with higher incomes would receive coverage quickly, while those in families with lower incomes would remain on waiting lists.

- Adopt supplemental report language directing MRMIB [Managed Risk Medical Insurance Board] to provide the Legislature with a quarterly report providing a statistical summary of the number of children placed on waiting lists, the period of time applicants must wait for coverage, and the effect of waiting lists on program enrollment rates. This information would enable the Legislature to assess the impact of the enrollment caps upon their implementation.

- Direct MRMIB to report at budget hearings on how conflicts with the CHDP [Child Health and Disability Prevention Program] gateway, parent expansion of Healthy Families, and SB 2 [Chapter 673, Statutes of 2003] should be addressed.

Source: Legislative Analyst Office, *Governor's Health Family Reforms: An Assessment*, February 18, 2004.

Apply the Twenty-Dollar-Bill Test

Before finalizing your decision, you should subject your favored policy alternative to the *twenty-dollar–bill test*, a good final check that your idea is indeed solid. The name of this test is based on an old joke that makes fun of economists. Two friends are walking down the street when one stops to pick something up. "What about that—a twenty-dollar bill!" he says. "Couldn't be," says the other, an economist. "If it were, somebody would have picked it up already." The analogy is this: *If your favorite policy alternative is such a great idea, how come it's not happening already? Why hasn't the proposal been enacted?* The most common sources of failure on this test are neglecting to consider the resistance of interest groups, bureaucratic and other stakeholders in the status quo, and the lack of an entrepreneur in the relevant policy environment who has the incentive to pick up what seems like a great idea, win political credit for taking an agreeable stance, and see it through. Failure on this test is not fatal, of course. You might keep fiddling until you invent a variant of your basic idea that will pass.

STEP EIGHT: TELL YOUR STORY

After many iterations of some or all of the steps recommended here—principally, redefining your problem, reconceptualizing your alternatives, reconsidering your criteria, reassessing your projections, and reevaluating the trade-offs—you are ready to tell your story to some audience. The audience may be your client, or it may include a broader aggregation of stakeholders and interested parties. It may be hostile, or it may be friendly. Your presentation may be a one-time-only telling, or it may be merely the first effort in a planned long-term campaign to gather support behind a legislative or executive change. (For a discussion of the issues likely to be involved in such a campaign, see Appendix C, "Strategic Advice on the Dynamics of Gathering Political Support.")

Apply the Grandma Bessie Test

Before proceeding further, however, you need another little reality check. Suppose your Grandma Bessie, who is intelligent but not very sophisticated politically, asks you about your work. You say you are a "policy analyst working for . . ." She says, "What's that?" You explain that you've been working on "the problem of . . ." She says, "So, what's the answer?" You have one minute to offer a coherent, down-to-earth explanation before her eyes glaze over. If you feel yourself starting to hem and haw, you haven't really understood your own conclusions at a deep enough level to make sense to others, and probably not to yourself, either. Back to the drawing board until you get it straight.

Now consider the possibility that someone might actually wish to base a real decision or a policy proposal on your analysis. (It's been known to happen.) Even if you, as an analyst, would not have to deal directly with such a tough audience as Grandma Bessie and her kin (including, of course, Grandpa Max), it's likely that someone will have to do so. At the very least, therefore, you'll have to be able to explain your basic story to someone in sufficiently simple and down-to-earth terms that that someone will be able to carry on with the task of public, democratic education.[46]

Gauge Your Audience(s)

Assuming that you've passed the Grandma Bessie test, identify and assess the likely audience(s) that are more sophisticated and involved than Grandma Bessie.

First comes your client, the person or persons whose approval you need most—your hierarchical superior(s), perhaps, or those who are funding your work. What is the relationship between you and your client? What you say and how you say it should depend a great deal on whether your relationship is long-term and on whether it is carried on face-to-face. In particular, how easy will it be for you to correct any misunderstandings that may arise?

Next, think about the larger political environment. Who do you think will "use" the analysis and for what purpose(s)? Will anyone pick up your results for use in an advocacy context? Would you regard this use of your results as desirable? Or desirable if certain advocates use your work and undesirable if others do so? Do you want to do anything to segregate the elements of your analysis by the type of audience you might want it to reach—or not reach? Are you, perhaps inadvertently, using scare words that will alienate certain audiences who might otherwise be open to your analysis?

If one of your goals is to engage a lay audience, keep in mind that ordinary folk are rarely moved by statistics alone. Indeed, relying on numbers to demonstrate the importance of addressing a problem can actually undermine the psychological processes needed to prompt a response; people may not only fail to grasp the statistics, but they may be numbed into inaction.[47] Data and statistics are obviously indispensable to analysis, but when it comes to telling your story to a general audience, be sure to put a human face on the problem. And show how your solution could make life better for real people.

If you are making a clear recommendation, make sure that you raise and rebut possible objections to it that might occur to various important audiences. Also, make sure that you compare it to what you or others might regard as the next best course of action, so as to be ready to show why yours is better.

Consider What Medium to Use

You can tell your story in written or oral form. In either case, communicate simply and clearly. The guiding principle is that, other things being equal, shorter is always better. In written presentations, good subheadings and graphics can make reading and comprehension easier.

Oral presentations require practice, self-discipline, and a little knowledge of some basic principles. The most basic of the basic principles are these: Speak *very slowly and distinctly*; speak loudly enough to be heard throughout the room, even over distracting noises; speak in a lower register, which tends to increase perceived trustworthiness and credibility; do not fidget, but don't stand like a stick, either; make lots of eye contact with audience members and, in doing so, don't favor one side of the room over another. Speaking slowly and distinctly is probably harder than you think—and more important, too. Visual aids such as PowerPoint shows often help in oral presentations.

An increasingly common medium for telling your story is the issue brief. The best issue briefs are short, crisp, and visually attractive. Issue briefs can be stand-alone documents, or they can be supplements to traditional written or oral presentations. Box I-10 shows an example of an issue brief from Research Improving People's Lives (RIPL). Note that the issue brief proposes the implementation of a randomized controlled trial, a rigorous scientific method to measure policy impact and effectiveness (see Appendix E). The issue brief is also an example of the "learning by doing" variant of multistage analysis discussed earlier in Part I.

Give Your Story a Logical Narrative Flow

Your story's flow should be designed with the reader's (or listener's) needs and interests and abilities in mind. In both written and oral presentations, it should be evident to the audience what motivates the entire analysis. Therefore, it is best to open with a statement of the problem your analysis addresses.[48]

It is also important to *motivate* the more detailed steps in the flow of the analysis—that is, the sections, paragraphs, and sentences. Most readers will look for the motivation of any element in what immediately precedes it, which makes it important to avoid lengthy digressions. For these reasons, be wary of sections that you are tempted to label "Background." Similarly, the phrases "Before turning to . . ." and "It is first necessary to explain/understand the history of . . ." are usually signs of undigested material. Many readers will be alert to these danger signs, so you should be, too. Policy analysis, remember, is about the future. Perhaps surprisingly—it is often not obvious how, or whether—history affects the future, but the burden should be on the writer or speaker to show exactly how this effect will come about.

A common, though not uniformly applicable, organizing framework is to begin with a good problem definition and then to treat each alternative you consider as a major section. Within each such section, you project the probable outcome(s) of implementing the alternative and assess how likely such outcome(s) are in the light of some causal model and associated evidence. Following these discussions, you review and summarize the alternative outcomes and discuss their trade-offs. This framework contains no special discussion of criteria; however, sometimes an explicit discussion of criteria is important. If so, it might appear either just before or just after the presentation of the alternatives and their associated outcomes.

Do not be afraid to start with a recommendation (if you intend to make one) and an assertion that, now that you have put it out, you intend to present all the necessary steps to justify it. You can often help the reader by providing a simplified, stylized account of a topic and then complicating it with additional details. You will find yourself writing (or uttering) sentences like "That is how a subsidy strategy will work if it works perfectly, but now we need to introduce

Box I-10 An Illustrative Example of "Telling Your Story" from a Policy Analysis Report

From: Research Improving Peoples's Lives, https://www.ripl.org/ wp-content/uploads/2018/08/RIPL_I3_Reducing-Recidivism-by-Connecting-Releasees-with-Social-Services.pdf

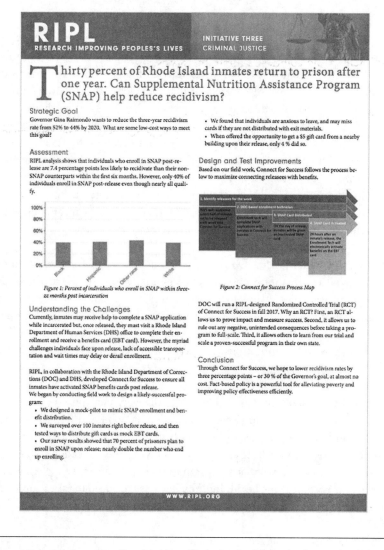

RIPL
RESEARCH IMPROVING PEOPLES'S LIVES

INITIATIVE THREE
CRIMINAL JUSTICE

Thirty percent of Rhode Island inmates return to prison after one year. Can Supplemental Nutrition Assistance Program (SNAP) help reduce recidivism?

Strategic Goal

Governor Gina Raimondo wants to reduce the three-year recidivism rate from 52% to 44% by 2020. What are some low-cost ways to meet this goal?

Assessment

RIPL analysis shows that individuals who enroll in SNAP post-release are 7.4 percentage points less likely to recidivate than their non-SNAP counterparts within the first six months. However, only 40% of individuals enroll in SNAP post-release even though nearly all qualify.

Figure 1: Percent of individuals who enroll in SNAP within three-zz months post incarceration

Understanding the Challenges

Currently, inmates may receive help to complete a SNAP application while incarcerated but, once released, they must visit a Rhode Island Department of Human Services (DHS) office to complete their enrollment and receive a benefits card (EBT card). However, the myriad challenges individuals face upon release, lack of accessible transportation and wait times may delay or derail enrollment.

RIPL, in collaboration with the Rhode Island Department of Corrections (DOC) and DHS, developed Connect for Success to ensure all inmates have activated SNAP benefits cards post release.

We began by conducting field work to design a likely-successful program:

- We designed a mock-pilot to mimic SNAP enrollment and benefit distribution.
- We surveyed over 100 inmates right before release, and then tested ways to distribute gift cards as mock EBT cards.
- Our survey results showed that 70 percent of prisoners plan to enroll in SNAP upon release; nearly double the number who end up enrolling.

- We found that individuals are anxious to leave, and may miss cards if they are not distributed with exit materials.
- When offered the opportunity to get a $5 gift card from a nearby building upon their release, only 4 % did so.

Design and Test Improvements

Based on our field work, Connect for Success follows the process below to maximize connecting releasees with benefits.

Figure 2: Connect for Success Process Map

DOC will run a RIPL-designed Randomized Controlled Trial (RCT) of Connect for Success in fall 2017. Why an RCT? First, an RCT allows us to prove impact and measure success. Second, it allows us to rule out any negative, unintended consequences before taking a program to full-scale. Third, it allows others to learn from our trial and scale a proven-successful program in their own state.

Conclusion

Through Connect for Success, we hope to lower recidivism rates by three percentage points – or 30 % of the Governor's goal, at almost no cost. Fact-based policy is a powerful tool for alleviating poverty and improving policy effectiveness efficiently.

WWW.RIPL.ORG

Source: Research Improving People's Lives, "Reducing Recidivism by Connecting Releases with Social Services," 2018. Reproduced by permission.

at least two sources of friction. One has to do with the likelihood that 5 to 10 percent of the claimants will probably be ineligible, and a majority of those may be fraudulent as well. The second source involves finding competent and willing partners in the nongovernmental organization (NGO) community to help with the outreach component." These sentences would prepare the reader for discussions of the ineligibility problem relative to the established scenario for working "perfectly," the political backlash if fraud were to become a big issue, and the complexities of partnering with NGOs.

Some Common Pitfalls

Following the Eightfold Path Too Closely. Occasionally, the Eightfold Path helps to structure your narrative flow as though you were leading the reader by the hand down its course. But this approach is almost always a really bad idea. It leads to a wordy, mechanistic product that repels rather than attracts the reader's attention. The purpose of the Eightfold Path, remember, is to help you *think through* a complicated problem. It is not necessary to use it in telling the story. Don't tell the reader about all the alternatives not taken and the many reasons why they were not. That's *much more* than the reader wants or needs to know. The reader should or would probably be interested in the weightiest reasons why one or two of the next-best alternatives are not recommended in preference to the one(s) that is (are)—but no more than that.

Compulsive Qualifying. Don't interrupt the flow of an argument in order to display all the qualifications and uncertainties about some particular element in the argument. A linguistic way around this pitfall is to use adjectives or adjective phrases, such as *most, on average,* and *more often than not,* to state the generality and then to return to the exceptions in the next section. (Or, if the exceptions and qualifications really can't wait, try a parenthetical sentence or a footnote.)

Showing Off All Your Work. Don't include every fact you ever learned in the course of your research. Even if you've done a good and thorough job of research and analysis, most of what you have learned will prove to be irrelevant by the time you're finished. That is, you will have succeeded in focusing your own attention on what is really important and in downplaying what only appeared important at the beginning. You don't usually need to take your reader on the same wandering course you were obliged to follow.

Listing without Explaining. Should you list every alternative policy that you intend to analyze in the report before you actually get around to providing the analysis? Such a list is a good thing when the alternatives are not numerous, when they are all taken seriously either by you or by your audience, and when they will prepare the reader's mind for the detailed assessment that will follow. However, if you have many alternatives to consider, the reader will forget what's on the list, and if some of the alternatives turn out to be easily dismissed upon closer scrutiny, you'll simply have been setting up straw men and wasting the reader's mental energy.

Similarly, be cautious about listing every evaluative criterion of interest before coming to the assessment of the alternatives being considered. Usually—though not always—not much can be said in a separate section about criteria that can't be better said when you're actually writing the assessment sections.

Spinning a Mystery Yarn. Start with the conclusion, the bottom line, the absolutely most interesting point you intend to make. Then present all the reasoning and evidence that you have to make your audience reach the same conclusions you have reached. In short, follow the opposite strategy from that which a novelist would follow.

Inflating the Style. Avoid the pomposity and circumlocutions of the bureaucratic and the academic styles. (Essential reading: George Orwell, "Politics and the English Language.") Also avoid a chatty, insider's style—such as "We all understand what fools our opponents are, don't we?"

Forgetting that Analysis Doesn't Persuade—Analysts Do. No matter how competent your analysis, it will be only as persuasive and credible as the person or organization who produces and communicates it. For oral presentations, the quality of public speaking matters; if you haven't taken a public speaking class, consider taking one. For presentations that will be televised or webcast, there are (nonobvious) dos and don'ts about how to look professional on camera; learn them.

Finally, remember that the persuasiveness and credibility of an analysis depends in no small part on the personal and organizational reputation of the analysts who produced it. If you or your organization produce a shoddy study, or appear unprofessional when you disseminate its results, the reputational costs may be with you for a long time. When you communicate an analysis, remember that you are not simply sharing your solution with the audience you are presently speaking or writing to—you are also building personal, political, and organizational capital to put yourself in the position to communicate other solutions—maybe even more important solutions—in the future. The LAO report excerpted in Box I-9 on the Healthy Families Program establishes credibility by acknowledging that a proposal it recommends against has virtues. Such credibility makes it more likely that the audience will be receptive to the analyst's story about why its preferred alternative is superior.

Structure Your Report

Unless the report is short, begin with an executive summary.

If your report is over fifteen to twenty pages long, say, a table of contents may well be helpful. If there are many tables and figures, either in the text or in the appendices, a list of these items can be helpful, as well. Detailed technical information or calculations should appear in appendices rather than in the text. However, enough technical information, and reasoning, should appear in the text itself to persuade the reader that you really do know what you're talking about and that your argument is at least credible.

Use headings and subheadings to keep the reader oriented and to break up large bodies of text; make sure your formatting (capital letters, italics, boldface, indentation) is compatible with, and indeed supports, the logical hierarchy of your argument.

Table Format. Current professional practice is very poor with respect to the formatting of tables. Do not imitate it but strive to improve it. Every table (or figure) should have a number (Table 1, for instance, or Figure 3-A) and a title. The title should be intelligible; it is often useful to have the title describe the main point to be learned from the table (e.g., "Actual Risks of Drinking and Driving Rise Rapidly with Number of Alcoholic Drinks—but Are Greatly Underestimated by College Students"). Each row and column in a table must be labeled, and the label should be interpretable without too much difficulty.

Normally, a table either is purely descriptive or is designed to demonstrate some causal relationship. In the latter case, it is usually desirable to create a table that makes a single point (or at most two) and that can stand alone without need of much explanation in the surrounding text. It is usually better to use two or three small tables to make two or three points than to construct one massive table and then try to explain its contents by means of the text that surrounds it.

Tables usually require footnotes, and there should almost always be a source note at the bottom. Sometimes these notes refer to data sources used to make the table, and sometimes they attempt to clarify the meaning of the row or column labels, which are necessarily abbreviated.

Please do *not* imitate academic practice, which is to overstuff tables with all kinds of numbers and to mindlessly apply obscure column and row labels. Academic practice presupposes that all the data have been gathered "scientifically" and without serious bias; therefore, the presentation style aims to convey these facts. Unimportant data share space in academic tables with important data so as to permit the reader to see that the complete truth has been told, that the author has not cherry-picked the data to convey only what is interesting and has conveyed the full story about what is statistically insignificant as well as what is. If these issues are important to you and your readers, by all means provide the full story. But do it in appendices. In most cases, though, try to minimize the information provided in a single table.

Statistics. Your audience probably does not understand statistics as well as you do, so keep your statistics few and simple. Percentages are good, and differences in percentages even better—for example, "The food budget for juvenile facilities serving boys (girls) is 10 percent higher per capita than that for facilities serving girls (boys)." If regression coefficients must be used, make sure the raw coefficients correspond to intelligible real-world phenomena rather than to mere index numbers that researchers have found useful. Intelligibility, moreover, always implies using metrics that are meaningful to your audience; for example, "A ten-cent tax on high-sugar foods would probably reduce per-capita consumption by 6 to 10 ounces per week." In this case, ounces per week is better than pounds per year or ounces per day, since yearly consumption means nothing to most people and most people probably suppose their daily consumption is highly variable whereas weekly intake smooths out the daily unevenness.[49]

References and Sources. Include a listing of references and sources at the end of the presentation. Books and articles should be cited in academic style (alphabetical order by author). The main point is to provide bibliographic help to curious or skeptical readers who want to track down references for themselves. There are several acceptable styles, but a good model is the one used in the book review section of the *Journal of Policy Analysis and Management*, which is simple and direct.

The current trend is toward "scientific citation" in lieu of footnote references in the text. That is, cite the author's last name and year of publication in parentheses in the text; the reader then consults the references section at the end for the full citation. If you follow this practice, the reference section should list the author(s) *before* the title of the work and other publication details, including the year. Sometimes you will want to include a page number in the parenthetical citation, as well.

Legal citation style is quite different. If most of the references are legal, then it is advisable to cite all references in bottom-of-page footnotes. However, you can keep the scientific citation format within the footnotes.

Notes are easier to read if they appear on the same page as the referenced text—that is, if you display them as footnotes rather than as endnotes.

Using a Memo Format

If your analysis is to be delivered in a memo, you should present it within a standard memo format, as follows:

[Date]

To: [Recipient name(s), official position(s)]

From: [Your name, position. Sign or initial next to or above your name.]

Subject: [Brief and grammatically correct description of the subject]

[The first sentence or two should remind the recipient of the fact that she asked you for a memo on this subject, and why. Alternatively, you could explain why you are submitting this memo on this subject to the recipient at this time.]

[If the memo is long, you might open and close with a summary paragraph or two. If you open with a long summary, the closing summary can be short.]

[If the memo is long, consider breaking it up with subheads.]

Develop a Press Release

Most policy analyses do not become the subjects of press releases or of radio or television sound bites, but some do. Others become candidates for such treatment, and all can profit, even in their extended form, from the analyst's reflecting on how to condense the essential message. Hence, it will probably serve an analytic purpose—and sometimes a political one—if you sketch out a press release or a few ideas for sound bites. You may also want to think strategically and defensively to see how an opponent might characterize your work in a press release or sound bite.

PowerPoint

PowerPoint slides frequently supplement oral presentations and indeed sometimes replace written reports altogether as nonverbal means of communication. Following are some brief comments on the use of PowerPoint; plenty of full-scale manuals are available.

- Keep it simple: have each slide present a separate point; use phrases, not sentences; and use only two or at most three colors.

- Choose text color and background color so that the text color is very legible on the background color.

- Avoid cutesy icons and "cool" moving animals.

- Think of the viewer's needs: to see letters and numbers at a fair distance, and to not be bored by having you as presenter simply read what is on the screen.

- Display the slide for long enough so that the viewer can actually read and absorb its contents—especially important for tables and graphs.

- Include slides at suitable intervals that summarize what has been said so far and point the way to what is yet to come.

- Make available to the audience, after the presentation—not during, as it is distracting—hard copies of slides (arranged six per page).

Visual supplements, such as photographs, can nicely support all the words, provided they are carefully chosen and displayed.

NOTES

1. See Roose (2018).
2. For an analysis of most traditional market failures in transaction cost terms, see Zerbe and McCurdy (1999), which also emphasizes the rich variety of interventions besides those undertaken by government to remedy traditionally conceived "market failures."
3. On choice architecture and social norms, see Goldstein, Martin, and Cialdini (2008) and Thaler and Sunstein (2008).
4. See Nyan et al. (2014).
5. See Oster (2018).
6. This happened to a graduate student group at the Goldman School whose client was the Oakland Police Department. Members of the group struggled hard to escape the initial assumptions held by their client and eventually to refocus their work.
7. Some analysts also claim that it is simply not worthwhile to define as "problems" conditions that cannot be ameliorated: "Problems are better treated as opportunities for improvement; defined problems, as problems of choice between alternative means to realize a given opportunity. The process of problem definition would then be one of search, creation, and initial examination of ideas for solution until a problem of choice is reached." See Dery (1984, 27).
8. Social scientists today are increasingly using rigorous experimental and quasi-experimental methods to identify causal relationships between variables, including randomized controlled trials, difference-in-differences, instrumental variables, and regression discontinuity. There are growing calls for government to use such research to inform policy analysis and evaluation. See Haskins and Margolis (2014).

9. Congressional Budget Office, *The Army's Ground Combat Vehicle and Alternatives* (report), April 2013.
10. These tips for finding creative solutions to problems are from Nalebuff and Ayres (2003). See also the valuable "nudge" approach in Thaler and Sunstein (2008).
11. For a good, brief discussion, see Stokey and Zeckhauser (1978) and Victorio (1995); also see the models, particularly that of case management, in Rosenthal (1982).
12. For other ideas and an excellent discussion of the uses of models generally, see Lave and March (1975).
13. Often, though not always, the basic element is something like a smart practice— that is, an intervention strategy that attempts to take advantage of some qualitative opportunity to create valued change at relatively low cost or risk. See Part IV, "'Smart (Best) Practices' Research."
14. Choosing a numerical target can help to focus energies and can force you to think about what effects are too small to be worth seeking. But when all increments are of equal value, choosing a target may be arbitrary and self-defeating.
15. Cost-effectiveness analysis is often used when the benefits of policy alternatives are difficult to monetize. For example, a Resources for the Future/National Energy Policy Institute study employed cost-effectiveness analysis to evaluate a carbon tax and cap-and-trade programs because of the difficulty of monetizing the benefits of reducing oil dependence and carbon dioxide emissions. See RFF/NEPI (Krupnick et al. 2010).
16. For a provocative argument that cost-effectiveness analysis is a better technique for most public purposes than benefit–cost analysis because the former looks away from individual preferences toward collectively established objectives, see Moore (1996, 35–36).
17. For an excellent textbook on benefit–cost analysis, see Boardman et al. (2011).
18. Karoly and Bigelow (2005, xiv).
19. We said earlier that criteria apply to outcomes and not to alternatives. However, this statement needs a slight amendment in the case of practical criteria, which apply not to outcomes but to the prospects an alternative faces as it goes through the policy adoption and implementation processes.
20. For an accessible introduction to this approach to the study of politics, see Shepsle and Bonchek (2010).
21. An analogous procedure was first given prominence by Graham Allison (1971).
22. On the implementation challenge of obtaining compliance among program targets, see Weaver (2010).
23. See Campbell (2012, 336).
24. See Patashnik (2008).
25. See Stokey and Zeckhauser (1978, chap. 11).
26. Also, in this case, the stem *respons-* appears in both alternative and criterion.
27. See p. 4, no. 7 at https://www.whitehouse.gov/sites/whitehouse.gov/files/omb/assets/OMB/circulars/a004/a-4_FAQ.pdf.
28. Congressional Budget Office, Letter to the Honorable Frank D. Lucas, September 16, 2013, https://www.cbo.gov/sites/default/files/hr31020.pdf.

29. This assumes that you do make a recommendation. But even if you only lay out options and attach projected outcomes to them, you still cannot escape justifying the projections.

30. Some people speak of "switchpoint analysis" and would refer to the 15 percent here as the "switchpoint" at which a decision-maker would switch from a favorable view of this policy to an unfavorable view or vice versa. Others refer to "threshold analysis" and would call the 15 percent figure the threshold level of effectiveness we would need to assume in order to justify choosing this alternative.

31. The example is discussed in Sunstein (2014, 75). Sunstein offers an excellent review of the uses of break-even analysis. Appendix D of that book provides a list of selected examples of break-even analysis carried out by the federal government.

32. A special case of break-even estimation is a fortiori estimation. If you hypothesize worst-case estimates of all important parameters that remain uncertain, and the policy alternative still satisfies your decision criterion, the alternative would, a fortiori, prove satisfactory even if more careful estimates were to be more favorable. In that case, the more careful estimates are unnecessary. See MacRae and Whittington (1997) on a fortiori analysis (218–219) and, more generally, on the question of precision versus approximation in projecting outcomes (209–224).

33. For further details, see Morgan and Henrion (1990, chap. 8). You can use the commercially available (and very user-friendly) Crystal Ball program to run Monte Carlo simulations.

34. Most of the work on this type of simulation has been done at the RAND Corporation. See Lempert, Popper, and Bankes (2003).

35. Doleac and Hansen (2016).

36. Ibid.

37. Doleac (2016).

38. Weaver (2009).

39. See Cryan et al. (2008).

40. They grouped their eight alternatives into five subgroups, however, to simplify the analysis.

41. Even when one policy alternative dominates other options, opportunity costs still must be faced. The implementation of policies nearly always requires the use of some resources that could be used to produce other things of value.

42. Confronting the trade-offs may require the analyst to acknowledge that certain negative outcomes are deemed to be acceptable, and not deserving of much weight, even if some people might be unhappy about them. For example, in the vaccination example discussed in Step One, authorities had to genuinely sacrifice the preferences of anti-vaccination parents who believe (erroneously) that vaccination causes autism. The analyst is thus deciding that the public's beliefs about vaccination are misguided and should count much less than the recommendations of scientific experts. Similarly, policy analysts might decide on the basis of science to regard climate change as a serious problem, even if this means ignoring the preferences of citizens who believe that climate change is a hoax.

43. Good discussions can be found in Adler and Posner (2001).

44. See Stokey and Zeckhauser (1978, 117–133) and MacRae and Whittington (1997, 201–203). One potentially misleading heuristic has the analyst creating a score for each alternative with respect to each criterion and then manipulating the scores arithmetically. It is easy to get the arithmetic right, but it is often hard to come up with scoring procedures that are not at some level arbitrary (e.g., anchored against some arbitrarily defined level of excellence or its opposite).

45. For reasons of space, we do not discuss the first of these matters here, but see Appendix B for a very brief survey of pertinent institutional issues.

46. Sometimes this is referred to as the challenge of giving an "elevator speech." You and your boss, or some relevant other, find yourselves together in an elevator for too long a time to make do with just "Hi, how are ya?" The boss asks how your project is going. You have maybe a minute to explain what you're up to and why he should be interested and perhaps persuaded. So have your elevator speech committed to memory and ready to go at a moment's notice.

47. See Slovic (2007).

48. An unusually fine manual on how to give slide-based oral briefings is published by the RAND Corporation (1994).

49. See Browner (2012). Although this is directed to academic researchers in medicine, much of the advice can easily be extrapolated to policy analysis.

PART II

Assembling Evidence

Consider the problems confronting you as a researcher preparing an analysis of water pollution control programs for Blue Lake. You know that there is a dirty lake; that federal, state, and local legislation is directed toward the goal of cleaning up the lake (or preventing it from getting much dirtier); and that a state environmental protection office in the area has something to do with administering some or all of the relevant antipollution policies or programs. But you need to know more. You need to map the present policies and programs, their political environment, the ways in which the bureaucracies function to implement them, and the criteria by which experts and nonprofessionals evaluate them. You also need to make some decisions about how *you* will evaluate them. Then, you need to learn what data are relevant to these criteria and figure out how to obtain these data. If you are planning to recommend changes in existing programs, you must develop the evidence that will permit you to make reasonable projections of the likely outcomes. In addition, you must learn what sort of changes the present set of relevant actors may be prepared to make or are capable of making.

These are large challenges, but your resources in time, energy, money, and the goodwill of potential informants and interviewees are probably not at all large. Moreover, you would like to finish the study in no more than six months, let us say, and you do not want to waste the first five months simply getting your bearings. Where are you to begin? And having begun, how are you to proceed efficiently?

GETTING STARTED

The first step is simple: Start with what you know. This injunction may seem self-evident or trivial or both. In fact, it is common for people to act in contradiction of it. Confronted by a new and challenging research task, they expect to flounder anxiously for a few weeks or months. And, behold, they do, for feeling stupid makes you so. Rarely is this waste of time and energy necessary, however. A few facts, or even vague recollections, plus some intelligent reasoning can usually move the project onto firm footing surprisingly quickly. Suppose, for example, that you are asked to do a policy analysis of "the future of the Wichahissic bituminous coal industry," a subject as remote from your interest or previous experience as galactic spectroscopy. You might take stock by writing a memo to yourself as follows:

- I was probably asked to do this study because someone thinks the future of the Wichahissic bituminous coal industry is pretty bleak or else because it is looking up. If the former, the results will probably be used to justify some sort of government subsidy; if the latter, the results will be used for promotional purposes by the industry itself or by local merchants whose livelihood depends on the health of the industry.

- The future of any industry depends in part on market demand. The demand for coal has probably been declining, partly due to the availability of substitute fuels.

- Maybe high production costs imperil the health of the industry. Could it be that coal-mining technology is underdeveloped? If so, why? Perhaps the coalfields are running out and the technology has not been developed to handle poor, as opposed to rich, deposits.

- There were a lot of miners' strikes a few years ago. Are labor-management relations better or worse now? Are wage demands forcing the companies to go under?

- Coal transportation depends on railroads. So, if the railroads are sick, could coal be sick as well?

- Coal is black and sooty, gives off a lot of smoke, and has a nasty carbon footprint. Surely this is an ecological menace. Who, if anyone, is paying attention to this problem? Or is it really a problem? Coal mining destroys the beauty, and probably the ecology, of the countryside. Is this really so? Might the Sierra Club have useful data on these questions?

- Perhaps not all coal is sick, just bituminous coal. Maybe the anthracite industry is flourishing. Surely there is a trade association of coal-mining companies with data here. Call up the nearest big coal-mining company and find out its name and address from the public relations office.

- Perhaps coal is okay, but Wichahissic has a problem. But then again, Wichahissic does not seem to be as much in the news as Pokanoka, whose plight seems to be the archetype for "the depressed area." Check Bureau of Labor Statistics (BLS) for unemployment figures here.

Writing memos of this kind to yourself is useful not only at the beginning of a project but also whenever you feel yourself beginning to drift toward panic or confusion. Following this initial stocktaking, you should think of yourself as designing, executing, and periodically readjusting a research strategy that will exploit certain predictable changes in your potential for gaining and utilizing information:

- *Locating relevant sources.* Over time, you decrease your uncertainty about what is worth knowing and how to learn it.

- *Gaining and maintaining access to sources.* (1) Over time, you augment your ability to arrange interviews with busy or hostile persons and to obtain data that are not clearly in the public domain; (2) over time, you also—and unavoidably—use up your access to certain sources, and you must therefore conserve such exhaustible resources for use only when the time is propitious.

- *Accumulating background information as leverage.* Over time, you improve your capacity to interpret data and to force them out of reluctant sources, thereby increasing your background knowledge.

- *Protecting political credibility.* Over time, the research process itself creates an environment that will either help or hinder the adoption and implementation of your—or your client's—eventual recommendations.

The optimal strategy for managing any of these problems may conflict with the optimal strategies for dealing with the others. Therefore, after each problem is discussed in a separate section as follows, the final section of this chapter is reserved for a brief treatment of the trade-offs involved in trying to meet all strategic imperatives simultaneously. We assume throughout that the reader is an inexperienced policy researcher who has had academic training in the social sciences. Hence, we go to some lengths, at various points, to allude to differences between social science research methodology and the methods of policy research. We trust that the more experienced researcher will also find some profit in the arguments here, if only to conceptualize more clearly what she has already learned to do intuitively.

A further clarification about the intended audience is in order. You start your task with certain resources and constraints, some of which are derived from your own experience and personality and others from your institutional location. Although institutional location is especially important in designing an optimal research strategy, it is not discussed in this book. Suffice it to say that the resources and constraints of a legislative staff assistant are quite different from those of her counterpart in a bureaucratic setting and are even more dissimilar to those of a student working with a campus-based Public Interest Research Group (PIRG). The strategic advice offered here is intended to be sufficiently general to meet the needs of researchers in any of these circumstances, however.

LOCATING RELEVANT SOURCES

Unlike most social science research, most policy research is derivative rather than original. That is, it is produced by creative play with ideas and data already developed by others. Only occasionally does the policy researcher set out to generate new data or assume responsibility for inventing a bright policy idea from scratch. Instead, the researcher's role is preeminently discovering, collating, interpreting, criticizing, and synthesizing ideas and data that others have developed already. To be sure, social science research often works this way, too, but it also places a much higher premium on originality. In a sense, the policy researcher becomes an expert on experts—those scholars and persons of experience who are thought to be relatively sophisticated about the policy area. (See also Appendix E, "Suggestions for Incorporating 'Big Data' and Rigorous Scientific Evidence into Policy Analysis.")

Consulting Both Documents and People

In policy research, almost all likely sources of information, data, and ideas fall into two general types: documents and people. By *documents* we mean anything that has to be read: websites, journal articles, books, newspapers and magazines, government reports, statistical archives, interoffice memoranda, position papers, bulletins, and so on. By *people* we mean anyone, whether a single individual or a group, who is to be consulted in person. Research on any policy problem usually entails a canvass of both types of sources.

Avoid the pitfall of overemphasizing one type at the expense of the other. Sometimes you fall into the trap out of habit: If you start out interviewing experts, experienced administrators, and other informed persons, you continue doing so until you come to define "interviewing" as what your job is all about. You forget that the experts themselves typically have obtained a good deal of their expertise by studying documents and that much of what administrators offer can also be found in agency reports, legislative hearings, published statutes and regulations, and so on.

Another reason for getting stuck in one medium and neglecting the other is an individual preference for less or more personal interaction—that is, for choosing to conduct your research via the internet or in libraries (or files, in an organizational setting) or for concentrating on fieldwork instead. But it is usually desirable not only to consult both types of sources (documents and people) but also to consult them in alternating order: a spate of interviewing followed by a retreat to the internet or the library followed by another round of interviewing, and so on. If for no other reason, there is probably a psychic economy in arranging and executing a fieldwork agenda in a consolidated time span, as there is in collecting and exploring a large body of documentary material.

In a more general way, however, one source should be used to locate another, and this branching out can just as easily lead from one medium to the other as it can from source to source of the same type. More explicitly, people lead to documents as well as to other people, and documents lead to people as well as to other documents. There are thus four basic branches on the tree of knowledge, each of which we discuss in turn.

People Leading to People. Often, one informant leads spontaneously to another by remarking during the course of an interview or a conversation, "Have you seen X yet? She's very knowledgeable about . . ." This information can be stimulated by your asking questions such as "Who else would be a good person to talk to about . . . ?" or the more specific "Who would be a good person to see in Agency Y?" For reasons of tact, you might frame the question more tentatively: "Do you think it would be advisable to talk to X—or do you think that would not be advisable?" Sometimes it is a good idea to ask the informant explicitly if his name can be used in seeking an appointment with the person he has suggested. This gives him an opportunity to protect himself if he does not want his name to be used and an opportunity to encourage name-dropping if he believes it will serve his interests. (That is, A may wish B to know that A has spoken of him as "a knowledgeable person," or words to that effect.) Make sure that the informant provides sufficient contact information for you to locate anyone he recommends seeing.

Knowing whom to stay away from is often an important by-product of inquiries such as these. If the informant is trusting and wishes to be helpful, he may volunteer a cautionary aside such as "If you do go to see X, you'll probably find her reserved if not unsympathetic." Unless X is a very important step in the developmental sequence at that moment, this may very well be a clue not to approach her until better groundwork has been laid for such a meeting. Another important by-product of such inquiries is a file of information on who is friendly, or antagonistic, to whom. Such information will be useful in constructing a map of political and administrative feasibility for any new program that you may eventually propose.

People Leading to Documents. Just as you can ask informants whom else to see or talk to, you can also ask them what else to read and how to obtain it. In visiting informants in their offices, you can sometimes get useful hints by scanning the bookshelves and the papers on tables and desktops for titles and authors or agency names. Also, take away from the interview all the documents that the informant is willing to give you, even if you are not sure how relevant they are. The chances are good that you will turn up some interesting new material in the collection you eventually develop, and, in any case, you may avoid a trip to the library should you later wish to quote these documents or to report precise bibliographic information. Finally, put yourself on mailing lists, so as to be on the receiving end of whatever stream of reports, bulletins, newsletters, circulars, and so on are distributed by organizations operating in the policy area. Many agencies keep budgetary and other numerical information in electronic spreadsheet form; ask if the files can be sent to you or, better yet, copy the files to a USB flash drive before you leave the office.

Documents Leading to Documents. Anyone who has ever written a substantial academic research paper in history or the social sciences has probably learned how to use one document to discover another through web links, footnotes, and bibliographies. The same procedures work in policy research. In addition, a researcher frequently uncovers references that are incomplete from a strictly academic point of view but that may still be useful for policy research. These include references to agencies or organizations (and even individuals) that have an ongoing responsibility for or interest in the policy area, some of whom can be expected to sponsor studies, reports, position papers, and so on that may prove invaluable.

Once research is under way, documents lead to documents in a relatively straightforward manner and without much difficulty. The problem is in knowing where to start when the research effort is just beginning. The easiest place to begin is the internet, where Google or some other search engine can be used to find the sites of advocacy groups putting forth their views of the problem and possible solutions. These sites probably contain valuable information and are a useful source of ideas and further leads. Because they are likely to be one-sided, however, you should try to find advocacy sites with opposing views.

But advocacy groups are just a beginning. More useful are the websites of policy think tanks, such as the Brookings Institution and the American Enterprise Institute (AEI). These are relatively mainstream institutions that produce large numbers of policy-relevant papers annually in almost all policy domains.

The best of these papers connect concepts from the social sciences (often by noted scholars) with applied problems, and they often provide an overview of some policy area. Brookings is sometimes said to be a "liberal" think tank and AEI "conservative." There is some truth in these characterizations, and the differences in the policy recommendations offered by think tanks on the mainstream left and mainstream right have increased in recent decades in tandem with the polarization of political elites, but such labeling is not as important as the fact that each of these institutions cares about its reputation for sound analytic work. It might be fair to say that they have political "orientations" rather than "biases." The same is generally true of the liberal Center on Budget and Policy Priorities, the conservative Hoover Institution, and the libertarian Cato Institute. In the environmental area, the leading think tank is Resources for the Future, which favors a benefit–cost approach to environmental policy. The RAND Corporation and MDRC are research organizations that produce high-quality policy analytic reports and program evaluations in many issue areas.

The websites of various governmental oversight institutions can be very helpful once you have in mind a particular legislative or regulatory issue. The Congressional Budget Office (www.cbo.gov) does hundreds of studies per year and posts many online. The Government Accountability Office (www.gao.gov) does the same.

Do not be satisfied with only the sites that are accessible by means of a public-domain search engine. If you have access to the online resources of a university (or governmental) library, use it. University or government-wide libraries typically subscribe to databases that can provide access to full-text newspaper and magazine articles (LexisNexis) as well as to abstracts and full-text publications in scholarly journals (JSTOR, in particular). *CQ Researcher Online*, published by CQ Press, provides access to feature-length journalistic articles dating back to 1991. *National Journal* is similar to *CQ Researcher*.

Because internet sources are so accessible, it is easy to forget about books (until the day they are all online, of course). Unfortunately, electronic search procedures do not work as well for finding good and appropriate books as they do for finding articles and relatively ephemeral materials. The best way to locate relevant book-length sources is to find out what the experts and advocates recommend. You can check the bibliographies in journal articles or—following the "people leading to documents" strategy—ask them.

Documents Leading to People. Once having read, or read about, the work done by certain experts, academic or otherwise, you may wish to consult with them face-to-face or by telephone. You should be wary, however, of mistaking the nominal author of a study for the real one, particularly when that author is a person or group in officialdom. The nominal authors of Supreme Court decisions, to take an extreme example, are the associate justices, but the real authors are usually their clerks, who in turn probably draw most of their arguments from the briefs filed by the lawyers on the case. Similarly, you should look behind the agency official whose name appears on the cover of a report, to locate the staff member(s) who did the work and may be named on the inside pages or referred to in a preface.

Seeking Secondhand Information

To find out what Senator A is doing or thinking about a policy problem, you need not necessarily ask the senator herself. Tens or hundreds of individuals may know the answer, or at least part of the answer. Such secondhand information must be used cautiously and checked constantly for bias or error. But it is not in any a priori sense inferior to information obtained firsthand, which may have its own biases and factual errors. To use a legal analogy, one relies for "truth" on witnesses rather than on the defendant, who, after all, cannot easily or prudently be asked to testify against himself. Sometimes it makes sense to obtain first-hand information as a supplement to the other, particularly if there is reason to think that failure to do so might ultimately jeopardize the credibility of the final research product.

The use of secondhand sources is especially important in seeking political feasibility data. Suppose, for example, that you are planning to recommend that emergency ambulance services be centralized under the city police department and you want to estimate the probable reaction of the fire chief to such a recommendation. You could ask the fire chief himself, but he might not be willing to tell the truth, especially if he were going to hold out his acquiescence in return for better terms or for some reciprocal benefit. That is, he might in principle be willing to go along with the change—he might even be enthusiastic about it—but for bargaining purposes he might not be prepared to say so. On the other hand, he might really be against it but not be willing to admit that, lest people call him an obstructionist. In either case, the fire chief is not a reliable source of this information. Eventually, it might be desirable to ask him his opinion directly, but you could probably learn as much or more by asking instead a variety of secondhand sources such as a veteran city hall reporter, rank-and-file firefighters, someone in the city manager's office, and someone from the police department.

Finding Multiple Sources of Firsthand Information

Suppose that you wish to know about the past relationship between the police and fire departments. Have they been relatively cooperative, antagonistic, or indifferent? If for some reason you do not wish to ask the fire chief, it is always possible to ask the police chief, since she has also been a partner to these relations. Her view or interpretation of the relationship may differ from that of the fire chief, but she is as much a participant and her knowledge just as direct.

This principle has numerous applications. If you want to know what happened at a particular meeting to which you were denied admission (or to which you could not go for other reasons), there are many participants to query. If you want to know how one particular participant behaved at that meeting, you do not necessarily have to ask that participant. You can ask others who attended. If you wish to see a memorandum sent by Smith to Jones, you can ask either Smith or Jones, depending on which one you believe will be more agreeable—or you can obtain a photocopy from a third party.[1]

Searching for Sources and Searching for Knowledge

At the beginning of a policy research project, you face a dual uncertainty: about what you think you ought to know and about where you can turn to learn it. These are interdependent questions, in the sense that the reduction of one type of uncertainty is both a consequence of and a condition for the reduction of the other.

Consider first what happens as you clarify your ideas about what you think you ought to know. Simultaneously, you are able to exclude certain sources you would otherwise have consulted, and because you know better what your objectives are, you are able to intensify your search for sources of greater relevance. This is the classic research model, in which ends determine means—that is, a constantly evolving set of knowledge objectives gives shape to the strategy of source selection and consultation. It is as applicable to policy research as to any other sort of social inquiry.

Its exact opposite is also applicable. Because the cost of searching for adequate sources is so high in time and energy, when you find a rich source it is wise to mine it intensively, even if that decision slightly alters your original knowledge objectives. If you wish to make recommendations to the state legislature concerning the reduction of criminal recidivism rates, for instance, the most relevant data source (recidivism in that particular state) may not be as rich—and therefore as useful—as data from the bureau of criminal statistics run by some state that does an especially good job of collecting such data.

One danger in this sort of pragmatism is that you may spend too much of your time on what appears to be a rich source, not knowing that there are much richer ones just around the corner. That is why it is wise to invest a good deal of time initially in canvassing a variety of possible sources and developing a broad overview of both the policy area and what means there are to learn about it. After this initial survey, it is possible to return to sources that look unusually rich. This procedure also guards against the second, and more important, danger in letting the sources guide you: You might lose sight of more desirable and feasible knowledge objectives. In the final analysis, there must be a balance between the classic model of ends (knowledge) dictating means (sources) and the pragmatic model of ends evolving out of the means one has at hand.

GAINING ACCESS AND ENGAGING ASSISTANCE

Gaining access can be a problem. If you wish to interview Assembly Member Jones, you must persuade Jones's appointments secretary that you are on serious business and that in any event you will not be put off. You must arrange an appointment for a not-too-distant date and persist even after Jones breaks the first appointment and fails to show up for the one made in lieu of that one. If you wish to interview Jones a second time, you must take pains to keep this possibility open and perhaps to foster it by your conduct during the first interview.

You may need to engage the active assistance of some informants, especially those who stand at the gateway to an agency's performance and budgetary data. Often these data are in a raw state—that is, the data are in the files but need to be collated and tabulated. Sometimes the data are in a semiprocessed condition; that is, they have been collated and tabulated, but they have not been put in a format intelligible to the researcher. (They are still in a format that is intelligible to the program managers, but this format does not fully reveal the meaning of the data to the researcher.) In such a case, you may wish to know about seeming inconsistencies in the classification of cases or about the meaning of certain class designations that the managers have developed for their own decision-making.

Finally, there are data that have been prepared for public use but have not been processed completely or adequately for your purposes. Suppose that the intramural evaluation staff of a state penal institution, for example, has issued its annual report on releases and recidivists, but you cannot tell from the report how reliably they have ascertained the prior arrest and conviction records of the so-called first offenders. Did they rely on probation officer reports? On prison records? Records from other states? The error structure of an agency's data is often not known to the agency, and if it is, it may not be made known to the public. In this case, as in the case of raw and semiprocessed data, interpretive assistance is needed from the agency itself. How much assistance it is willing to give may depend, in part at least, on how well you have established rapport with the agency and its personnel.

Getting an Appointment

Why should any informant grant you, a mere policy researcher, an interview? American manners and mores provide the most compelling reason—it is part of our definition of courtesy. If someone talks to you, even through your appointments secretary, you are supposed to talk back. Of course, the more powerful, busy, or politically defensive the personage besought, the less will be the force of simple courtesy. In such cases, you might try to appeal to a sense of noblesse oblige or, if you have a prestigious institutional affiliation, to a willingness to exercise your caste privileges. In addition, many people simply feel flattered by the interest of an outsider—even a policy researcher—who wants to listen to them.

More reliable than these appeals to courtesy or vanity, however, is an appeal to political self-interest. Try to indicate that the outcome of your research is likely to have a bearing on the interviewee's (or her agency's) political fortunes and ambitions. It would therefore be prudent for her to be cooperative, to arrange for you to hear her (or her agency's) point of view, and indeed to use the interview setting to assess the relevant political implications of your work. Of course, it may require some fast-talking over the telephone, when you call for an appointment, in order to set her mind thinking in these directions. In dealing with an appointments secretary, who will probably be even less sensitive to your political cues, you may have to make your points indelicately explicit. Instead of relying on the vagaries of a telephone conversation or an appointments secretary, it may be useful to write a letter requesting an interview, followed up by a telephone call.

Your informants will often be acquainted with one another and will occasionally talk among themselves about you and your work. Since you want such discussions to serve your interests rather than to work against them, you should try to develop a reputation as a competent, knowledgeable, and energetic researcher who is likely to produce something of intellectual or political significance. The best way to develop such a reputation is actually to be such a person, but, in addition, certain stratagems may prove useful. Attempt, for instance, to become a familiar face, by attending meetings and conferences that your potential informants attend and by loitering around office cafeterias or after-hours places that they frequent. Try to impress people with your ability to gain entrée to meetings that are only quasi-public in nature and by talking in public places to important personages. All this familiarity will backfire if you appear pesky or inept, so some judiciousness is in order. Also, you should appear to be learning quickly and critically while in these settings, rather than observing passively and dully. A notebook or laptop computer, in which you enter notes fast and furiously, is a good stage prop as well as useful in its own right. Likewise, animated conversation, preferably observed rather than overheard, can enhance your appearance in these settings. But do not be indiscreet by becoming a bearer of information from one interviewee to another.

Fieldwork does not proceed rapidly or smoothly. For the most part, you are a hostage to other people's schedules. You can expect delays of several days to several weeks between the time you request an appointment and the appointment date—and even longer if your informant eventually breaks the appointment and reschedules it for a few weeks later. (Sometimes it seems that research is mainly idle waiting!) This problem is particularly acute if delay in seeing one informant becomes a bottleneck to seeing others. To minimize idleness, it is a good idea to have two or three independent streams of interviewing running simultaneously, so that a bottleneck in any single stream cannot halt your work altogether.

Cultivating Access

Securing repeated access to an individual or agency presents different problems from securing a one-time-only appointment. Courtesy is of almost no use here; the political motive, conversely, is critical. Since the political impact of your work on certain individuals and organizations will almost certainly be adverse, some doors will inevitably be closed to you. Beyond a certain point, there is nothing to be done about them, except to seek alternative means of entry. A perceived political affinity helps, but not much. Repeated access depends, instead, on building personal rapport. This takes time, especially if you are not inclined to appear more friendly and congenial than you really feel. Rapport follows most of all from simple exposure. Think of yourself as an anthropologist who has to spend several months living among the tribe you are studying before being allowed to observe certain sacred rituals and practices.

At the risk of sounding patronizing, we will nevertheless note here that the researcher should observe the basic courtesies. Be on time. Dress appropriately, which generally means with the same degree of formality as the interviewee or just a little less. Be friendly without being overly familiar or presumptuous. If you tape interviews—always a good idea, in order to preserve a record—set up your equipment with minimal fuss and explain that the tapes are for your own reference only. State that you will turn off the tape whenever the informant wishes you to do so.[2]

Almost invariably, whoever actually assists you in collating and interpreting agency data will see himself as "doing you a favor," regardless of how insistent his superiors have been that he make his services freely and generously available to you. As part of the protocol for such a favor, you must reciprocate with expressions of gratitude for his "going out of his way." An even more cooperative informant might mail you a copy of a speech she has recently given, knowing that it will be of interest to you. Or she might see to it that you are put on the list of invitees to a banquet at which you will be able to meet a number of potential informants in an informal setting. To a certain extent, this sort of assistance can be encouraged simply by letting people know that it will be welcomed. It can be facilitated by offering telephone and fax numbers or email and postal addresses where you can be reached or where messages can be left for you. It may even be useful to have business cards printed with this information; relative to other research expenses, this one is quite small and can return high dividends.

Exhausting Access

Access can be exhausted, too, not just cultivated and built up. Whereas in some cases repeated exposure helps the researcher to build rapport, in others exposure simply tears it down. In the extreme instance, one exposure is all the relationship will bear; this commonly occurs when the informant is defensive or antagonistic or when she is extremely busy and cannot easily be imposed upon. Other instances are intermediate: The informant is willing to grant two but not three interviews—or three but not four. When you suspect that access to an informant may be exhausted relatively quickly, defer interviewing her until later in the research process, principally because your accumulated knowledge will then support a more productive interview.

Usually, deferring interviews with such informants inflicts no hardship on the researcher, since in the earliest stages, research can be conducted by talking with the legion of lower-level officials and administrative assistants, public relations officers, and so on. Potentially useful information sources are to be found among retired officials and among agency officials who are part of a dissident faction.[3] These are rich sources at any time, but they are especially valuable in the early stages of research when it seems advantageous to defer your approach to more highly placed figures in the political establishment.

The researcher's reputation is also susceptible to being exhausted. It is perhaps not in danger of being lost, strictly speaking, so much as it is vulnerable to being transformed into a liability. Instead of being thought of as fair-minded, discreet, intelligent, and self-possessed, you may begin to be regarded as a partisan, a talebearer, a dope, or a dupe. The best way to avoid acquiring such an undesirable reputation is to eschew partisanship and indiscretion and, as we have already indicated, to actually be intelligent and self-possessed.

CONDUCTING A POLICY RESEARCH INTERVIEW

Policy research, in its completed form, becomes a political resource. Whatever its merits or demerits as a piece of rational analysis, it amounts to more than that. It may become a justification for certain parties to attack others or to defend themselves against attack and, hence, can be a weapon of persuasion in a war of propaganda. Although the tone and the format of published policy research are typically neutral and disinterested, everyone recognizes that the research may be and often is used for political purposes, either by the author or by others. As a result, informants are highly sensitive to the political implications of whatever they tell you. How an informant treats you depends in large part on how she thinks your work will be brought to bear on her personal or political interests.

Being wary of the possible political implications of what they might reveal, informants may be reluctant to talk freely and honestly. You should assume that all interviewees confront this problem, even though you may not know to what degree. In more extreme cases, it may be necessary to use various subtle kinds of leverage against the interviewee. Before turning to the problem in its most severe forms, though, we will sketch a basic strategy for conducting policy research interviews in general.

Energizing and Steering the Conversation

The interview process is an interaction carried on between the informant and yourself. In this process, the principal source of energy should be the informant. Your tasks are, first, to encourage the informant to talk and to keep on talking and, once a suitable momentum has been attained, to steer, to redirect, to slow down, or to cross-examine.

In addition to the political motivation, informants will talk because they have a story to tell. It is safe to say that many politicians, administrators, and important staff feel (correctly) that much of their best and most valuable work, which is being done behind the scenes, is unnoticed and underappreciated. They will be surprisingly eager to use you as their conduit to the outside world. Some also want to make their "side of the story" better understood than they think it is—and, if you haven't heard it from others yet, you may be surprised at how interesting it is.

In most social science research involving interviews, it is assumed that the interviewer is, as much as possible, a neutral instrument for recording data emitted by the respondent. However, this is generally an inappropriate model for policy research interviews. Here the informant assumes that you as an interviewer are anything but a neutral instrument—and it would be foolish for you to try to appear in such an ill-fitting disguise—since the whole object of your research is to arrive at some policy recommendations. Thus, you need not fear probing the informant with provocative and even argumentative questions or comments—or to answer such questions in return. Such exchanges can cause an informant to sharpen her wits and tone up her memory, and they may raise her psychic metabolism sufficiently to infuse energy into the whole interview process. If this is done with proper finesse, the informant will appreciate the stimulation. Your finesse as an interviewer, of course, consists of being argumentative without sounding (or being) closed-minded or hostile. It is a good idea to introduce contentious remarks in such a way that the informant, should she wish to do so, can retreat gracefully from the matter at hand into another topic—thus keeping her energy level up rather than dropping into an embarrassed reticence.

Most interviews are conducted at the informant's place of work. Sometimes, however, a more informal public setting, such as a restaurant or café, should be chosen. Your method of note-taking should be compatible with such an informal setting—perhaps on the back of an envelope handily stored in your pocket for just such occasions.

Apart from energizing the informant, your other main function in the interview process is to steer her onto topics of interest to you. How can this be done?

Sometimes you must interfere in the informant's conversation stream simply to reestablish your right to speak, temporarily slowing down the informant without making her lose too much momentum. This can be done by interrupting with a short string of easily answered factual questions pertaining to the subject matter she has been discussing. The content of these questions, or at least the last one in the string, should be suitable to work as a transition to the next topic you have in mind. Suppose, for example, that you are interviewing the integrated-social-services coordinator in your county, who is telling you about her agency's relations with the county's chief administrative officer (CAO). Having heard enough on this subject, you now want to steer her onto her agency's current budget request to the US Department of Housing and Urban Development (HUD). The conversation might go like this:

Informant: So you see we've had a devil of a fight with the CAO all the way. Maybe it's not her fault, of course, the Board of Supervisors being so conservative and the CAO needing support for her reappointment—

Researcher: [Interrupting] Yes, she is up for reappointment this year, isn't she?

Informant: Yes.

Researcher: Well, at least she doesn't control your budget, does she?

Informant: True enough.

Researcher: But HUD does—and how are your relations with them? Do you get pretty much what you ask for from them, in the way of a budget, I mean?

The point is not to disguise from the informant the fact that you are trying to steer her away from one topic and onto another, although sometimes this is desirable and should be attempted. The point is really to help her move from one topic to another without having to lose momentum or to feel awkward. Indeed, she will sometimes feel trapped on a topic that she herself would prefer to leave, and your job at such moments is to help her maneuver off the subject. If you cannot think of where you wish to lead her next, just think of a subject that is not implausible and that is not too demanding emotionally or intellectually. While you go in slow motion through that topic, both you and the informant will have a chance to collect your thoughts and feelings preparatory to moving to the next matter of serious concern.

Involving an informant in discussions of personalities is a delicate matter. The informant must be reassured that you are not turning the interview into a gossip session, that she is not a purveyor of gossip, and that you are not a seeker of it. This can be done by first introducing the name of the personality in a neutral, usually factual, context:

Researcher: A few moments ago you mentioned the Southside Community Health League. Dr. Green has been head of that for about a year now—or is it two?

Informant: Probably closer to two.

Researcher: Maybe it just seems shorter because I remember Dr. Black, his predecessor, so vividly.

Informant: Yes, Black was quite a leader there.

Researcher: Seems people have been more critical of Green—though I have heard quite complimentary things from some sources.

Informant: Yes, he's pretty controversial. He is certainly a competent administrator and has been pretty nice to us—though we deal mainly with his deputy, Mr. White.

Researcher: How come?

Thus, the conversation is turned to personalities by a sequence of small steps, in which each participant encourages the other and in which both assume responsibility for whatever gossipy quality may eventually threaten to intrude. Since personalities are such a sensitive topic, it is even a good idea to sprinkle your conversation with allusions to people about whom you may have no desire to question the informant. When you do want to pursue a discussion of a particular personality, this procedure makes the discussion seem less of a departure from the normal course of topics.

If the informant has unpleasant things to say about the personality under discussion, you may want to take pains to establish your own social, personal, and political distance from that individual. In the example just given, for example, the researcher has referred to "Dr. Green" rather than "Bill Green" and has indicated his distance by suggesting that he is unfamiliar with certain particulars of Green's career. If the informant has flattering things to say about the individual in question, you may choose to follow a contrary course, though it is always a little risky to appear very close to anybody, lest it arouse suspicions of partiality.

Leveraging the Defensive Informant

Occasionally, you encounter an informant who is irrevocably committed to a defensive posture, for whom "No comment" is the primary safeguard and calculated evasion is the fallback position. Try to diagnose this problem very early in the interview and then reassess your goals for the interview in light of it. Concentrate on gaining information about specific questions that this informant is able to answer but that are probably not answerable by any other source. Since so much of your energy will have to go into cracking the informant's defenses, focus on some very specific objectives and begin to probe for them right away.

Once these preliminary assessments are out of the way and the interview has turned to specifics, the use of leverage is in order. First, let the informant understand that you are aware of his defensive posture, and signal that you do not intend to be put off by it. You might try to communicate that his defensiveness will not help him, that you know too much already to be shunted aside, and that you have access to other sources who have already told you much and to still others who will be willing to tell you more. Indicate that information from these sources may be more prejudicial to his interests than his own revelations would be and that he therefore has nothing to lose, but perhaps something to gain, by giving honest answers. A certain amount of bluffing may sometimes be necessary, though this tactic carries obvious risks. It is always better to actually know as much as you pretend to know and to have access to the sources you claim to have access to, than merely to bluff.

Here is a sample of such an interview, with the head of a prominent local insurance company whom the researcher is pressing hard:

Researcher: One thing I'd like to get more information about is the problem insurance companies have writing policies for merchants in so-called ghetto areas.

Informant: [Silence. Pause.]

Researcher: I mean, there may be problems because these policies are risky business propositions.

Informant: [Silence. Pause.]

Researcher: People say they are risky, anyway. Do underwriters in this area consider them risky?

Informant: I can't really say for sure.

Researcher: Well, some people in the Black Merchants Association claim that insurance companies won't write policies for them at all, that they've been classed as "unacceptable risks."

Informant: I don't really know—insurance underwriting is the science of risks, isn't it?

Researcher: [Deciding that informant will provide no information on insurance industry doctrines or practices in general, or on the local underwriters in particular; guessing that informant will be unwilling to discuss the doctrines or rules applied by his own company and deciding therefore to concentrate solely on gathering information about the practices of the informant's company.] Perhaps I can clarify my question by being more concrete. In your own Bedrock Casualty Company, are applicants ever turned down because they are thought to be unacceptable risks?

Informant: I can't say for sure. I'm not that close to the operating details of our very large company.

Researcher: Of course. [Signaling she will not be put off.] You, or perhaps your secretary, could arrange for me to talk to someone at that level, though, couldn't you? [Seeking a different leverage point.] But tell me about the category of "unacceptable risks." Does Bedrock Casualty tell its salespeople that the company will insure any premises provided the insured pays a high enough premium? [Shifting the terms of the question to throw informant off guard.] Or is there a limit on how high a premium the company will set?

Informant: Well, we do not like to charge exorbitant premiums, of course—

Researcher: [Interrupting.] So within the existing limits on premiums, there might in fact be businesses too risky to insure—hence "unacceptable"? [Holding to offensive.] How about cancellations? Has Bedrock canceled or refused to renew any policies of ghetto merchants even though they have not filed any claims recently? This is another thing the Black Merchants Association has been complaining about.

Informant: [Deciding researcher knows more than he had thought and seeking preemptive protection against the Black Merchants Association's allegations.] Well, yes, we have canceled a few, in the more riot-prone areas, and refused to renew other policies in that area. We had no choice; we stood to lose a lot of money in case of any trouble.

Researcher: [Graciously ignoring this "confession," and trying to induce the informant to tell his side of the story.] Of course, that's quite understandable. I think most people recognize this problem. [Now taking aim on a single statistic, the proportion of all Bedrock policies in "ghetto" neighborhoods canceled or not renewed in the last two years.] In the past, have you written many policies in that area?

Informant: Yes, we've done quite a bit, in the past anyway.

Researcher: You still do insure some business over there, don't you?

Informant: Yes, we do, though as I say, I'm not too close to the operating details—

Researcher: [Interrupting.] Could you estimate what proportion of your policy holders from, say, two years ago you continue to insure? Is it 80 percent, 20 percent? Just to give me some rough idea.

Informant: Well, it would certainly be a lot closer to 80 than 20, but I really don't know.

Researcher: [Deciding that this would be an interesting datum and that it is worth pursuing vigorously.] Can we find out?

Informant: Not easily. It's not in any files anywhere in that form, and it would be awfully difficult to find out.

Researcher: [Not believing that it would be very difficult; deciding to contribute her own labor to searching the files, if necessary; and resorting to a bluff.] People have the impression that Bedrock is less inclined to write policies for "ghetto" merchants than other companies in this area. I don't know where the facts come from— but I think some lawyers connected with the Black Merchants Association have been looking into legal aspects . . .

Informant: What? I'm sure we are no worse, or different, than any other company in town! I'd like to see these so-called facts!

Researcher: If I get any further clarification on that, I'll be happy to let you know. Meanwhile, I'll be willing to help out in whatever way you like in getting this information together concerning your own company's record in this field.

Let us interrupt this scene without a conclusion because, however it turns out, the researcher has done the best she could. The president of Bedrock Casualty may deliver the information sought, or he may not. Good interviewing strategy and tactics do not guarantee success, especially when the odds are weighted against the researcher to begin with.[4]

One common ploy used by a defensive informant is to reel off masses of irrelevant statistics and facts, which can easily swamp a naively data-worshipping researcher. Another ploy is to ramble garrulously about side issues, while running out the clock on whatever time limit has been set for the interview. Your best defense against these evasive tactics is to be able to recognize them for what they are.

If your own leverage fails—and if the elusive information is sufficiently important to you—you may be able to use someone else's. A graduate student researcher may have little leverage with determinedly defensive bureaucrats, for instance, but a legislator or her staff assistant will almost certainly have more. Hence, as a last resort, you might persuade a sympathetic legislator to help out. Sometimes a newspaper reporter or an established group can be of assistance. The local medical society, for example, may be able to get information from the county hospital administrator about hospital policies that no academic researcher—and perhaps not even a county supervisor—could get.

A significant constraint on using leverage is the desirability of maintaining cordial relations with whatever agency or individual is being pressured, for you run a clear risk of alienating the objects of your leveraging tactics. With respect to a given study, this problem can be mitigated by postponing the more offensive tactics until relatively late, when the study is less vulnerable to being undermined by the offended party. The problem is more difficult, however, when you envision a long-term relationship—lasting well beyond the conclusion of the present research effort—with the agency or individual under scrutiny. Certain information may have to be sacrificed in order to preserve a modicum of goodwill for the future.

USING LANGUAGE TO CHARACTERIZE AND CALIBRATE

The basic medium of the interview is spoken language embedded in a conversational context. Such a medium, when used as a representational device, presents reliability and validity issues (in psychometric terms).

Semantic Tip The simplest issue—to see, though not necessarily to resolve—involves the language of characterization. If an informant says, "Yes, this is a frustrating job," you have to interpret both the nature and the intensity of the word *frustrating* and do so in a way that permits you to calibrate the result against some larger frame or benchmark. This can be done by asking a series of questions designed to do the calibrating. One shortcut is to start by offering up your own characterization and see how the informant reacts to it: "If I had this job, I would find it awfully frustrating, I think." This quickly establishes a benchmark of some kind—"awfully frustrating"—for you and the informant to use. Of course, there is the problem of knowing whether you and your informant mean the same thing by the expression, since your frustration thresholds may differ. But you're off to a good start.

An improvement on the previous example would be to create two such benchmarks—that is, to describe a whole continuum with anchors at both ends and perhaps a verbal midpoint. For example, you might ask, "Would you say that your reaction to proposal X was extremely skeptical—as I've inferred from what you already have said—or was it relatively favorable . . . or was it maybe 'wait-and-see'?" This approach has the added advantage of respecting virtually any position your informant holds and of communicating your willingness to find anchoring words based in the informant's own history. Or you could anchor one or both ends in what "other people" have supposedly been saying.

To be sure, by characterizing the available options in this way, you are putting words into other people's heads and sometimes into their mouths. Before you proposed "X was extremely skeptical," your informant may never have thought of the proposal in this way, and so you run the risk, by asking the question, of having created such a thought out of thin air. But that risk comes from using language as a medium; it can't be avoided. Even when you use the ostensibly neutral and clinical language that survey researchers and reporters use, you are putting words into people's heads and mouths. More provocative characterizations, when used as benchmarks, are on a logical par with the more neutral alternatives offered by survey instruments and professional journalists.

PROTECTING CREDIBILITY

Like social science research, policy research is eventually subject to criticism on intellectual grounds. But unlike social science research, it is even more vulnerable on political grounds and, indeed, is vulnerable to attack by the very subjects of the study. In social science research, the subjects rarely become significant critics of the product, but in policy research, their criticism is inevitable. Therefore, the researcher should take steps to protect the ultimate political credibility of his work from politically motivated as well as strictly intellectual attack.

Defending against Politically Inspired Criticism

In contrast to that of social science research, the primary goal of policy research is not intellectual enlightenment (either yours or that of your professional colleagues), although enlightenment is inevitably a by-product. Instead, the goal is to improve your understanding of a policy problem, and of possible means of coping with it, to the point at which it becomes possible to advocate a responsible course of action. Thus, policy research takes aim at broad and complex phenomena, and so it is typically satisfied with very gross approximations of "truth," in contrast to social science research, which typically seeks more refined interpretations of narrowly circumscribed problems. The gross and approximate character of policy research is an open invitation to politically inspired criticism. How can you, as the researcher, protect yourself?

For one thing, you should attempt to touch base with any party (or any institutional interest) who might later try to undermine the report by claiming to have been ignored. Indeed, it is a good idea to preempt such claims by quoting that party in the report, as evidence of a sort that the party's views were taken into account. For instance, if you are going to recommend alterations in the way superintendents are selected in a given school district, it would be best to interview representatives from the local association of school administrators and from the local chapters of the National Education Association and the American Federation of Teachers. Spokespersons for these groups may have interesting opinions to contribute to the research project, but even if they do not, by consulting them you gain protection against their criticisms should they decide to oppose the recommendations in your report. It may even be useful to send out a preliminary copy of the report to these interests for reviews.

Second, you should seek out "experts" or others with political or intellectual authority to whom you can attribute views, opinions, estimates, and so on, about which you feel especially uncertain. Quoting published sources is one way of making such attributions, and including quotations from interviews is another. In addition, you should line up experts who will be willing to speak up in support of your work once it becomes public. Sources who are quoted in the report as having a view on this or that subject become natural targets for inquiring journalists or political decision-makers; these sources have an incentive to defend their quoted views when questioned.

Third, you should pay special attention to potential opponents and identify which propositions they are likely to attack. These target points should be bolstered in advance by expert quotations, and some polite reference should be made to the existence of counterarguments—without giving them too much space or prominence. The very opponents who can be expected to raise objections later should be quoted, to defuse any claims that their arguments or positions were ignored. (There may be additional psychological advantages to the balanced or two-sided presentation, simply as a subtly persuasive form of propaganda directed at the reader.)

Statistics can be useful for buttressing credibility. Employed for this purpose, they play a documentary rather than an informational role. Statistics can document the validity of generalizations that political opponents might otherwise challenge, even though their truth is abundantly evident through more impressionistic sources.

Preparing for Premature Exposure

Politicians and policy researchers work on different timetables. The former often call for "results" well before the research is in any sense finished. Even when no one demands it, however, unexpected opportunities often do present themselves before your research work is close enough to being finished that you can seize the auspicious moment to present your results.

One possible strategy is to map out (as much as possible) the timetable of potential political demands and to arrange your research timetable in at least partial correspondence. Another strategy is to prepare yourself as soon as possible with answers to the crudest kinds of questions that might be asked of you. Since these are generally the kinds of answers politicians need and want anyway, you may as well formulate them early in the course of your research. Finally, it is important, early on, to line up your supporting experts, as well as to touch base with potential opponents. Since, once again, these contacts must be made eventually, there is good reason to make them sooner rather than later.

STRATEGIC DILEMMAS OF POLICY RESEARCH

By way of summary and conclusion, let us consider a question: Which informants should be approached when? Answering this question forces a useful review of most of the issues discussed earlier.

We may divide the "when" part of the question into "relatively early" and "relatively late" in the course of the research project. Approach the following informants relatively early:

- Persons who are likely to facilitate your search for rich information sources

- Powerful persons who directly or by your reputed connection with them will facilitate your access to sources

- Knowledgeable persons who will provide you with the information you need to hedge against premature political exposure of your work and whose information will contribute to your capacity to exert leverage against defensive interviewees

- Friendly experts who will contribute to your political credibility in case of premature political exposure

- Potential opponents with whom you touch base in order to hedge against premature political exposure

Approach these informants relatively late:

- Hostile or defensive informants against whose tactics a prior buildup of leverage is desirable

- Busy informants to whom you might lose access permanently once you have seen them, or about whom you are not sufficiently informed to interview early

- Potential opponents, especially if powerful, who might try to forestall your access to others and thereby cripple your research efforts

- Administrators who have knowledge of potential trouble spots but who will be unwilling to point them out until it appears to be in their self-interest

There is one obvious contradiction between these two lists—approach potential opponents early and late—and several others that are not quite so obvious. Often the busy and the defensive informants are also in the best position to facilitate the search for sources, open doors, and provide useful information. Top agency administrators, for instance, may have plentiful experience with the policy problem under investigation and may be able to provide easy access to sources, but they also have a vested interest in maintaining the status quo or something very close to it. In any event, they may not take kindly to having their activities scrutinized too carefully by an outsider. Other similar examples can easily be called to mind. There is in principle no way to reconcile these incompatible prescriptions of whom to approach early and whom late. You will have to consider the full details of your particular situation and then balance the risks and rewards inherent in any given choice. There is no way of avoiding such trade-offs; you should simply make them consciously rather than inadvertently.

NOTES

1. The notion of systematically using secondhand sources and the notion of finding multiple sources for firsthand information are foreign to the spirit and practice of much social science research, which typically assumes that when you want to know the mental states or the conduct of a given individual, the best source is that individual. Such a researcher then worries about how to devise measuring instruments and interviews that will register these facts about the individual with the least distortion. Often, this is quite appropriate for the questions requiring basic and original research, when the object is to get pure data for pure understanding. But in policy research, the problem is to get a sufficient understanding of the world to be able to make estimates about alternative courses of action. Since there is much uncertainty about the future, and so many uncontrollable variables that will enter into future action, too much precision about the past and present frequently gets in the way.

2. If you come to sensitive material in the interview, remind the interviewee of your earlier offer to turn off the tape recorder.

3. Former Goldman School colleague William Niskanen observed that colonels twice passed over for promotion to general were a favored source for civilian policy analysts like himself in the US Department of Defense.

4. The researcher's bluffing tactic in this scene is of debatable morality. Although we believe it would be unethical in most circumstances, there are occasions when it can be justified. This is one of them. In this case, the Bedrock president seeks to withhold proprietary information. Does he have a right to do so? Normally, yes. But this right has to be weighed against the injustice of depriving ghetto merchants of a nearly essential prerequisite for doing business when they might be perfectly willing to meet reasonable price terms for acquiring the insurance (perhaps with government or philanthropic assistance). The researcher here has an arguable right to try to combat this injustice. Given that right, does she also have the right to use deception? The use of explicit deception on the part of the researcher is balanced by the use of implicit (covert) deception on the part of the insurance company's president.

PART III

Handling a Design Problem

This handbook assumes throughout that you are working on a discrete problem of policy choice. Your focus is on understanding the problem and analyzing the menu of potential solutions. The conceptual space in which you are working is relatively constrained because you are trying to identify the best way to intervene in an otherwise workable system. A special case of policy choice arises, however, when the system itself is functioning poorly—or when no system exists at all. Now you face the challenge not simply of analyzing an existing menu of alternative interventions but of adding to the menu as well. You are about to become a designer.

Design challenges are everywhere. Most challenges in "exploiting opportunities," as opposed to solving problems, also involve designing some relatively fresh or new system. For example, perhaps the college you work for is doing a perfectly respectable job of educating students and producing research but is missing an opportunity to harness the expertise and volunteer capacity of faculty to help the local community develop an action plan for improving the regional environment.

Perhaps you are just not satisfied with the menu of alternatives that people in the policy environment are already talking about. Or perhaps you believe that the wrong goals are being pursued. You might think that the criminal justice system should focus less on punishment and more on preventing people from becoming criminals in the first place. Or maybe you think the focus of analysis should be not on how to improve the outcomes of existing interactions among people but on how to change the nature of those interactions themselves. Perhaps the relationship between labor unions and local manufacturing plants has become too formal and adversarial after a worker was seriously injured on the job, making it impossible to build mutual trust, gather facts about the current rate of workplace injuries, and develop options to promote occupational safety.

Design challenges may arise when it seems impossible to find an alternative that will actually satisfy all important criteria—including political feasibility and implementation robustness and adaptability—without the support of many other inputs or processes, which may themselves be in need of augmentation or repair. If you are working on a problem of improving educational outcomes of children from disadvantaged backgrounds, one option might be to give extra homework to children who are not making adequate yearly progress in school. But maybe this works only if the supplemental assignments actually get done each night, and that would require the active support of the students' parents, many of whom work multiple jobs and lack the ability or time to provide the requisite level of monitoring and engagement. A second option would be to reward teachers on the basis of the learning outcomes of low-income students. But adopting such a policy without changing social policy more broadly could punish teachers for problems beyond their control and potentially push the most talented teachers toward schools serving more affluent students. It may be impossible to identify a simple intervention that will make a significant and lasting difference to learning outcomes for disadvantaged children; changes are needed not only in what happens in the classroom but also in the coordination and mutual expectations of parents, social service agencies, and the school system. Hence, the policy designer may be signing up to conceive of a more complex intervention, which is almost surely going to bump into constraints of its own.

IT'S A PRODUCTION SYSTEM

Think of yourself as designing a system that, in its eventual steady state, will produce a set of desired outcomes such as heating oil vouchers in the hands of needy homeowners or new residential electric outlets to service a growing fleet of electric autos or teenagers who plausibly have been diverted from a subsequent life of crime. The production process involves technical and human elements such as teachers, children, electrical current, curb space, oil tanks, and transportation vehicles. It also involves administrative and political elements such as budgets, outreach programs, guidelines, eligibility rules, a screening capacity, rules for appeals and for making exceptions, and so on. These elements must be assembled, fashioned into an operating system, properly managed, and competently defended against waste, fraud, abuse, and assorted political threats: the policy designer has a big job.

Actually, the designer has two jobs. The first is to fashion a system that, when up and running, will produce what it is supposed to produce in its steady state. The second job is to plan a strategy of political and bureaucratic change that will take us from here to there. The first job is predominantly technical; the second predominantly political and bureaucratic. In this part, we discuss the first of these jobs at length and the second briefly and only at the end.

CROSSWALKS FROM THE EIGHTFOLD PATH TO "SYSTEMS OF ACTION"

Design entails lots of trial and error. That cannot be avoided. But there are worse things than trial and error—for one, spinning your wheels for hours and days trying to find "the best" starting place. Besides, making mistakes at least gives you something to learn from. You can, for instance, improve your map of where the blind alleys are, so you won't go down them again.

Trial and error comes in two main forms, constructive and thrashing about. The latter is magnified when groups, not just individuals, are doing the problem-solving work. The Eightfold Path helps you to thrash about less when dealing with conventional policy analysis problems, and it can help with design problems too. We need to look for "crosswalks" and a few of the more helpful paving stones.

DEFINE THE PROBLEM ➡ FOCUS ON A PRIMARY OUTCOME

Complexity is your main enemy, so start by simplifying. The two main routes to simplifying are by means of outcomes and by means of constraints.

Although any system you design will probably need to produce several different outcomes, pick one such outcome, frame it in quantitative terms, call it "primary," and start by focusing on it. Figure out the best way to achieve it, note the limitations this implies as well as the pathways this seems to open up, and then fill in the blanks with respect to the rest of the outcomes. If this starting place later proves to lead nowhere, shrug your shoulders and try again.

The other main way to simplify is to start with constraints, especially one that looks very nasty. Maybe you can't breach an existing, important contract, for instance, and that may be unfortunate for your problem-solving abilities. In the real world, constraints—budgetary, say, or political—are annoying. But there is an upside to constraints in the mental world of policy analysis—they shrink the options you will need to explore. The irritations that come when faced by some difficult constraints may be just what you need to simplify overly complex decision and design problems and open your reservoirs of creativity—necessity being the mother of invention. Constraints are so useful, in fact, that sometimes it is desirable to assume they exist at the start of an analysis even though you know that at a later point you will relax that assumption and get more realistic. Here are some examples:

- "The governor has asked our task force to come up with a strategy for dealing with Problem X. Okay, let's suppose we have $5 million to spend on Problem X over the next three years. What should we spend it on?"

- "Okay, let's suppose that number is $15 million, not $5 million. Suppose we stay with our conclusions about that first $5 million. What should we do with the next $10 million?"

- "It's impossible to deal with Problem Y without making some of the current stakeholders very angry. Suppose we assume a political tolerance for any policy choice of, at most, one thousand voters who show a likelihood of greater than 50 percent of switching from support to opposition in the next election."

- "Or suppose we assume that, at most, we can jeopardize $100,000 in campaign contributions."

Just as you should try to quantify the definition of the problem, you should quantify the definition of the primary outcome. Quantification focuses the mind and the analytic objectives. The desired, and quantitatively specified, outcome for, say, a new electric vehicle subsidy program could be an average of five thousand vehicles per year in a five-county region, give or take a hundred. Your first effort at design might prove to result in only three thousand. No problem. Just go back to the drawing board and see how this can be scaled up. You already know how to get three thousand, so all you need to do now is find a way to add two thousand. That might involve extending the geographical domain for outreach activities, increasing the subsidy, loosening the rules for eligibility, or somehow partnering with county governments on electrifying vanpool fleets.

CONSTRUCT THE ALTERNATIVES ➡ CONFIGURE THE SYSTEM'S ORGANIZATIONAL STRUCTURE AND ITS OPERATING PROCESSES

Your initial step is important, as the design process is somewhat "path dependent." Your first step influences your choice for a second step, the second step is a prelude to the third, and so on.

Hunch and experience are probably more important in making the choice of a first step than any strictly logical or analytic guidance of which we are aware. Consider the following possibilities:

- *Start with the least flexible design element.* If you want to promote mass transit but there is a tight budget constraint that probably forecloses purchasing new rolling stock, you know you should focus your attention on people and behavior.

- *Start with the most "powerful" design element.* By *powerful*, we mean that the element, once chosen and its likely value assumed, strongly suggests the next most important element to consider. Once those two elements are chosen, the rest more or less "naturally" fall into place. To do this, you need a realistic theory of cause and effect that, to some extent, links the various elements. Although a perfect theory is probably lacking, some rough guesses can usually suffice. In the mass transit case, we would guess that supplying disincentives to single-occupancy auto use, in the form of tolls or congestion fees, would probably be the best place to begin, the theory being that mass transit use depends on making private autos a comparatively less desirable mode of transportation. That theory could also suggest making mass transit more attractive, perhaps by decreasing fares. But our own hunch is to start with disincentives to auto use, which we suspect would be more powerful than making mass transit marginally more attractive. Of course, on inspection, the opportunities for increasing the costs of auto use on targeted routes might be too few to make much difference.

- *Start with the most robust element.* Since there is always a possibility that the complete, and ideal, system will never come into being— politics and budgets being volatile and uncertain—it might be a good idea to put something in place that would be socially valuable all by itself. This might, for instance, be some sort of limited set of elements (a subsystem, one might say) involving discounted bus passes for employees of large traffic generators.

- *Start with the most transitory, and least costly, element.* We are thinking here of grant-in-aid windfalls that typically come from a higher level of government and that might, by design or by accident, disappear in a year or two.

Check Your Assumptions as You Proceed. The trial-and-error process requires, first, creative imagination and, second, rigorous evaluation of what creative imagination comes up with. The most commonly applied evaluative procedure is to generate what are known as *logic models*. This involves spelling out in some detail, and often with the help of graphic aids, how the emerging system is supposed to work. Presently, a leading source of ideas about how to do this is the W. K. Kellogg Foundation *Logic Model Development Guide* (available online at www.wkkf.org/resource-directory/resource/2006/02/wk-kellogg-foundation-logic-model-development-guide).

The Kellogg Foundation's approach is to divide the planned program or, in our language, *system* into five parts: resources/inputs, activities, outputs, outcomes, and impact. The modeler is supposed to fill in the details in each category and to specify the assumed relationships. In general, this approach assumes a production model, in which services of some kind are being delivered to a recipient population by a governmental or nonprofit organization. The model can be applied to nonproduction systems too—for example, regulatory systems—provided one is creative enough at filling in the "activities" section, which is supposed to work—but doesn't always—as a catchall for the complexity of relationships among system elements.

Another, very similar, approach, designed explicitly for service systems, is *service blueprinting*. It goes somewhat beyond logic models in that it also asks the modeler to specify assumptions about "offstage" and back-office support functions.[1]

Designing a Case Processing System. Design problems are generally of two types. One involves the management of "cases," by which we mean individuals or other entities (such as firms or communities or lower levels of government) that receive some kind of "treatment." The treatment may involve delivery of a subsidy, regulatory imposition of obligations, or application of some sort of person-changing regime (such as educating children or getting offenders to "go straight"). The second principal type of design problem involves operating on a collectivity of some kind rather than on individual cases—for example, improving traffic flow, eliminating corruption in the police department, preserving habitat, or launching a community cleanup campaign.

The second type is too varied to discuss here, but the first type, a program that manages cases, fits a rough template. That is, we can lay out a general procedure and list questions that should be asked. We use the term *program* deliberately, to refer to an organized ensemble of routines. For instance, a program to distribute subsidies has routines for determining eligibility, calculating the amount to be paid, and detecting and deterring fraud and abuse. A regulatory program has routines for enforcing compliance with its rules, including inspection procedures and formulas for applying sanctions. It may also have routines for adopting rules, giving technical assistance to regulated parties, and offering forbearance in exchange for more efforts to cooperate. In a person-changing program, the routines typically bring the subjects into a setting where change is to be rewarded, facilitated, induced, or demanded and where professionals apply a whole kit of tools to the change process. Think of schoolchildren, classrooms, and teachers; or of patients, hospitals, and doctors; or of welfare recipients, training programs, and caseworkers and trainers.

The logic model and service blueprint approaches can work for these types of programs, but each approach needs to be amplified to take account of three design levels: the individual, the population, and the managerial system. Presumably, the analysis has to be done for each of these three levels separately. The short version is (1) understand, in all its complexity, how a single representative case would be handled by your design; (2) scale up to understand how the program might handle a moderately large population of moderate heterogeneity; and (3) when at scale, understand how such a program might be competently managed. For instance, in a weatherization program, design issues at the individual case level might involve rules covering eligibility, what sort of weatherization measures to use in a particular type of dwelling unit, copayments (if any) that the agency charges the customer, and what sort of guarantees (if any) to provide the customer regarding performance. At the population level, another set of design issues intrudes, such as which type of customers to target, how to allocate weatherization-counselor time among target groups, whether to manage counselors by geographical districts or by types of functional expertise, how to handle customer complaints, and the like. At the management level, the designer must figure out such matters as how to create and sustain efficient information flows, how to train counselors, and how to draw up and justify budget requests, among others.

Look Around. But where might you get all your good design ideas in the first place? Take advantage of design efforts made by others before you. Perhaps the problem you are dealing with is so new or unique that you will be the first, or even the only, person to oversee the needed design work. More likely, though, others have already dealt with a problem that is similar, at least on certain key dimensions. It pays to see what they have done and to assess their degree of success or failure. Successful approaches are usually the most helpful, but sometimes you can learn a lot from evident failures, as well.

Where would you look? It may help to observe sister jurisdictions or institutions. If you are thinking about a problem at the state level, look to other states; at the city level, to other cities; at the community foundation level, to other community foundations. Professional associations linking governmental officials (such as chief of state school officers, district attorneys, or county welfare directors) often publish materials describing "best practices" in one or more of their member jurisdictions; even if they do not, a phone call to the executive offices of the association may produce useful leads.

When you are looking around, however, you may need to consider whether the problems in your "target" jurisdiction and the "source" jurisdiction are similar in nature and scale. A city that has nearly solved its homeless problem with a service-rich mix of supportive housing and solicitous outreach (e.g., Philadelphia) may or may not be a source of good ideas for a city with a problem that is four or five times as large per capita and has a physical climate that is very mild and therefore attractive to homeless people (e.g., San Francisco). You may discover that although the source's ideas are very good indeed, they will need to be adapted to the target jurisdiction's particular context. (For more on how to deal with this "extrapolation problem," see Part IV, "'Smart (Best) Practices' Research.")

A Little Help from Your Friends—and Enemies, Too. In some cases, the policy analyst works on the design problem more or less alone, like some brooding master architect. More likely, she does her work in loose or tight conjunction with other policy professionals who bring to the table different sorts of expertise (e.g., legal, engineering, fiscal) and who bring different viewpoints and priorities, as well. In any case, sooner or later, the design work will be held up to much more public view. Interested stakeholders, and perhaps more diverse audiences, who have previously been unaware of the design work going on seemingly behind the scenes, will see what you're up to. And they will offer their reactions.

You will want to use such reactions for two purposes: to improve your design according to criteria that you and your client—and very likely your audiences—think are important, including the criterion of political feasibility; and to respond in such a way as to increase the political support (and decrease the opposition) that may come your way, now or later, on process grounds alone.

We do not discuss here the strategy and tactics involved in communicating effectively with different audiences or the sequence in which to do so. We limit discussion to the questions of just how rough or polished the design should be that you first subject to relatively public review and comment and how tentatively you should put it forward.

Not surprisingly, a middle ground is best. An overly rough and admittedly tentative design may leave out important points, creating a sort of vacuum that outside interests will rush to fill on their own terms. You will then be forced onto the defensive, as you try to forestall the solution they have been first to suggest. Moreover, a very rough design may signal that the design work is at such a preliminary stage that it is not worth the trouble (or the risk of early mover vulnerability) for any of the stakeholders to react at all. On the other hand, an overly polished and seemingly definitive design may signal to stakeholders that you are not interested in consulting them. In that case, they may feel that they have no choice but to oppose your design more vehemently than they otherwise might have done—unless, of course, they conclude that they have no choice but to get on board and negotiate for the best terms they can manage.

At a more analytic level—because any design must be anchored in working assumptions about its objectives, available resources, and constraints—you should choose your assumptions with an eye to their reasonableness as "a basis for further discussion." You may feel some discomfort at putting forward such assumptions because they are hypothetical or speculative and because critics might, therefore, challenge them as "lacking in rigor." Policy analysis is not just an exercise in truth telling, however. It is a pragmatic and responsible effort to facilitate reasonable discourse about a policy future that is inherently uncertain.

A common set of design issues revolves around making adjustments—sometimes large, sometimes small—in an existing organization or interorganizational network, so as to improve performance. Space precludes discussion here of this vast set of topics, but Appendix B, "Understanding Public and Nonprofit Institutions," provides a menu of questions that any analyst of organizational performance issues ought in most cases to consider.

SELECT THE CRITERIA ➡ DEFINE THE OBJECTIVES TO BE ACHIEVED

We distinguished previously among criteria that involved maximizing certain conditions, satisfying conditions, and conditions for which "more (or less) is better." Outcomes or objectives fall into the same three categories. In addition, there is a fourth category in the design case, meeting the target level for whatever serves as your primary objective—for example, getting five thousand new electric vehicles on the road per year for the next five years.

In conventional policy analysis, the primary evaluative focus is on whether or not a projected outcome will solve the policy problem to an acceptable degree. A conscious explication of the objectives to be achieved may or may not show up among the criteria. In a design problem, however, finding ways to satisfy articulated objectives is the whole point of the analysis. It is important to keep going back to basics, to reiterate to yourself and others the main objective of the program. What latent opportunity is supposed to be seized? Or what existing program is to be redesigned to accomplish what objective better? Doing so presents an opportunity to think also about an often-neglected but very important design issue of a more instrumental kind: What evidence will you systematically collect in the course of normal program operations that can let program managers know whether they are succeeding? That is, what tracking and evaluation routines can be designed and put in place?

PROJECT THE OUTCOMES ➡ TEST WHETHER IT WILL WORK

Of course, you cannot know for sure whether the system, once up and running, will actually produce the targeted outcomes at an acceptable cost and in a reasonable time and with a tolerable amount of waste, fraud, and abuse. Mental testing is needed, and not only by you. Involve your friends and allies.

The test should be like a "stress test," now familiar in the world of banking regulation. Have a devil's advocate participate, a party that tries hard to think of ways to defeat or abuse the envisioned system—a party, that is, who can think with "a dirty mind."

CONFRONT THE TRADE-OFFS ➡ EXAMINE THE SYSTEM FROM MULTIPLE PERSPECTIVES

After developing one or two design ideas, the analytic task is to compare them to one another and to other design possibilities that are being considered by other parties, if such exist.

In confronting the inevitable design trade-offs, it helps to look at any set of routines from multiple perspectives. Try to put yourself in the shoes of each actor, and ask how well the system would work from her perspective. For example, in the case of a social service program delivery design, consider both the perspective of the case manager in the agency and that of the citizen whose case is being "treated." It often happens that routines designed to make life easier for program staff only make life harder for citizens. ("Sorry, we don't give advice about that; send in the application and we'll respond …") Remember that trade-offs occur at the margin. In this example, we would like to know this: If we spend an extra X dollars to allow program staff to spend Y more hours weekly responding to requests for advice, will we get Z more units of citizen satisfaction with the agency or fewer than Z units?

DESIGN A TRANSITION STRATEGY

Once you have designed—on paper, in your mind, and perhaps in the minds of all your friends and political allies—a system that is believed to have a reasonable chance of working in an eventual steady state, it is time to think about the transition problem. How do you get from here to there? This is too vast a topic to discuss here in any detail. We leave you with only one prescription: figure out who would best be suited in terms of both motivation and potential influence to act as champion of this design for the next few years; then, do what you can to ensure that they will take the job and have, or can get, the resources to carry it through. The champion can be an individual, a political coalition, an agency, an elected official, or a professional network. Unfortunately, just because you have worked so hard on designing a beautiful policy system, you can't assume that, once you depart the scene, the beauty alone will bring the system into being and make it work well.

NOTE

1. A good source of information about this approach is Bitner, Ostrom, and Morgan (2008).

PART IV

"Smart (Best) Practices" Research

UNDERSTANDING AND MAKING USE OF WHAT LOOK LIKE GOOD IDEAS FROM SOMEWHERE ELSE

It is only sensible to see what kinds of solutions have been tried in other jurisdictions, agencies, or locales. You want to look for those that appear to have worked pretty well, try to understand exactly how and why they may have worked, and evaluate their applicability to your own situation.[1] In many circles, this process is known as "best practices" research. Simple and commonsensical as this process sounds, it presents many methodological and practical pitfalls. The most important of these is relying on anecdotes and on very limited empirical observations for your ideas. To some extent, these are—one hopes— supplemented by smart theorizing. This method is never perfectly satisfactory, but in the real world the alternative is not usually more empiricism but, rather, no or thoughtless theorizing. Part IV helps you to avoid the pitfalls and offers tips on how to get the most payoff from your search for best practices.

DEVELOP REALISTIC EXPECTATIONS

Semantic Tip First, don't be misled by the word *best* in so-called best practices research. Rarely will you have any confidence that some helpful-looking practice is actually the best among all those that address the same problem or opportunity. The extensive and careful research needed to document a claim of best will almost never have been done. Usually, you will be looking for what, more modestly, might be called "good practices."

But even this claim may be too grand. Often, you can't be sure that what appears to be a good practice is even solving or ameliorating the problem to which it is nominally addressed. On closer inspection, a supposedly good practice may not be solving the problem at all. Inadequate measurement, plus someone's rose-colored glasses, may simply be producing the illusion of problem mitigation. It may also turn out that, even if good effects have truly occurred, the allegedly good practice had little or nothing to do with producing them. All these are known technically as *internal validity problems*. The discussion that follows assumes such problems have been satisfactorily—though not perfectly—resolved and concentrates only on the *external validity problem* of extrapolating from a setting in which a good practice has indeed worked well to settings that differ in little-understood but important ways that may lead to weak, perverse, or otherwise damaging results.

ANALYZE SMART PRACTICES

A *practice* is a tangible and visible behavior. When you can ask a program manager what her practice is in addressing some problem, she can answer with a description of what she does. Typically, though, a practice is also an expression of some underlying idea—an idea about how the actions entailed by the practice work to solve a problem or achieve a goal. Some such ideas are particularly clever, and we shall explain further what we mean by this. The practices that embody them we call "smart practices."

Finding the Free Lunches

One way of being clever is by getting something for nothing. Contrary to the dictum that there is no such thing as a free lunch, creative policymakers and policy implementers invest quite a lot of energy in looking for just such comestibles. Often, they are successful. To understand how this can be, consider the free lunch cornucopia produced by the natural sciences and engineering. The energy stored in the chemical bonds in a cup of gasoline can run a car for a few miles if only you know how to access that energy and channel it. Pulleys and levers supply mechanical advantage. Bacteria happily eat and destroy the organic crud in a city's wastewater almost for free. All these materials, devices, and conditions amount to getting a lot of "something" for nothing or for relatively little. The source of all these boons is simply Mother Nature.

In the social world, the sources of something for nothing are usually less tangible and less directly gifts of Mother Nature, but they are no less real. The "invisible hand" of the market creates social value where once there was only individual pursuit of self-interest, and, metaphorically at least, it operates without charge. Alphabetical ordering permits people to find information in a fraction of the time it would take were there no such ordering. Queuing at bus stops is easy to understand and usually fair, and it makes life better for everybody.

In the world of policy and management, there are no doubt fewer and less delectable free (or nearly free) lunches than in the marketplace or in an information storage facility or at a bus stop. But they are there. All the "opportunities" described in Box I-1 (see Part I, under Step One, p. 10) have this latent potential to generate something of public value relatively cheaply. (On the nature of "public value," see Moore 1996.) You might say that the difference between the (high) value created and the (low) cost, and risk, of producing it represents a free lunch.[2]

Opportunities don't deliver up their latent value without some additional work, however. This work is done by practices that take advantage of their potentialities, and these practices typically cost something and are subject to various vulnerabilities, as well. However, the smarter these practices are, the more value they can manage to extract at lower cost and risk.

The following list offers some examples of candidates for smart practice status—candidates, that is, because to our knowledge they have not been subjected to the extensive empirical testing needed to confirm such status:

- *A "high-expectations" welfare-to-work program.* Implemented in the early 1990s, the Greater Avenues for Independence (GAIN) program one of us studied in Riverside County, California, was a prototype for the 1996 federal welfare reform act. Unlike most other welfare-to-work programs, the Riverside program set high expectations about work for GAIN participants in two senses. In many different ways, it signaled to participants that program staff had confidence in (high expectations of) their ultimate success in getting a job and getting off welfare. This confidence was intended as an antidote to many participants' low self-esteem and consequently low effort to reattach themselves to the labor force. Staff also signaled—and expressed in program rules about early and diligent job search, as well as through a variety of formal and informal pressures—that "society expected" welfare participants to shape up and take responsibility for their own financial well-being. The Riverside GAIN program designed its recruitment, training, performance appraisal, and other administrative systems to support this high-expectations philosophy (Bardach 1997). In effect, the high-expectations model took advantage of the natural energy to solve their own problems that program managers assumed to be latent in the program participants.

- *Reading One-to-One.* This tutoring program for children in Grades 1–3 who have fallen far behind in learning to read English was created by George Farkas, then of the social sciences faculty of the University of Texas at Arlington. It was first tried out in Dallas and then spread to Houston and a number of other cities. The program involves systematic instruction in phonemic awareness, one-to-one tutoring by a well-trained tutor, and highly structured feedback and supervision. Like all phonemics-based programs, it recognizes that English orthography does not map sounds in a systematic or logical way and that it is at some point necessary for learners to master the decoding and encoding rules actually in use. It takes advantage of the fact that children's early failures in reading that come from neglect of phonemic awareness are reversible by regular tutoring. It also takes advantage of the emotional bonding that comes from the one-to-one tutoring relationship and of the increased motivation after the student experiences some successes. The simplicity and systematization of the teaching materials, teaching methods, and administrative oversight system make the program easily replicable and keep the costs relatively low (Farkas 1998).

- *Sharing maintenance responsibilities for a neighborhood park.* The local parks department and the residents of the neighborhood share these responsibilities. Nonprofit organizations often spring up to provide services of a nonstandard sort not provided by the public agency (e.g., same-sex schools, abortion clinics). An extension of this basic idea is a partnership in which the public sector supplies certain resources that are not only supplementary but also complementary. In many a setting, the city government provides the parkland and the neighbors provide some or all of the labor to make the land more serviceable in some way. This practice takes advantage of two interesting potentialities: the potential for gains from trade between two parties and the use of what is in effect bartering, in a situation where there are administrative and political barriers to organizing the transaction in cash.

- *The "expenditure control" budget.* Adopted first in the city of Fairfield, California, this practice was publicized by David Osborne and Ted Gaebler (1992) in their influential book, *Reinventing Government.* As originally conceived and implemented, this budgeting strategy gave each department the same basic mission and the same budget as in the previous year (with an inflation adjustment) but abolished the line-item specification of expenditures, permitting the department to keep any savings and reinvest them in other mission-related activities. This approach took advantage of the superior technical and operational knowledge of program implementers relative to that of elected officials and bureaucrats in fiscal-control agencies.

- *Milestone payments to nonprofit service contractors.* In 1992, the Oklahoma Department of Rehabilitation Services began paying nonprofit contractors for meeting rehabilitation milestones, defined in performance terms, that mental health clients could achieve en route to higher levels of employability.[3] The clients participated in assessing whether the milestones had been met, and the contractors helped to define generic milestones and other aspects of the program. The milestone system also permitted contractors to claim reimbursement from the state on a more accelerated schedule than they had previously been able to do, thereby taking advantage of the power of self-interest to motivate better performance from the nonprofits. It also provided greater transparency than more traditional fee-for-service arrangements, under which the funding agency did not know much about the quality of the service provided.

- *A cooperative project between rehabilitation and recycling programs.* Hennepin County, Minnesota, arranged for county vocational rehabilitation program clients with intellectual disabilities to sort and recycle discarded auto batteries, an item of concern to the county's environmental management agency.[4] The two programs thus took advantage of production complementarities between human and physical "assets" that they could deploy.

Semantic Tip We have made a point, in describing supposedly smart practices, of saying that each practice "takes advantage" of something. This is a linguistic device for ensuring that, in analyzing how the practice works, we focus on how the practice aims to exploit, or take advantage of, some latent opportunity for creating value on the cheap.

Breaking Loose from Conventions and Assumptions

Another way of being clever is not so much technical—finding those free lunches—as ideological and psychological. It involves disrespecting conventional boundaries. In the world of public policy and management, this practice sometimes involves challenging assumptions that are anchored in value commitments. For example, since the late 1980s, policymakers have begun to shake loose the assumption that just because some good or service is "good for the community" and ought to be *financed* through taxation, it ought also to be *produced or delivered* by government employees. Instead, we now contemplate contracting out to the nonprofit or even the profit-seeking sectors such traditionally "governmental functions" as primary education, correctional institution construction and management, and welfare-to-work programming.[5] In this case, we are challenging the assumption that governmental provision necessarily embodies a social expression of the value of community. Taxpayer financing may do so, but governmental provision does not.

Another value-oriented smart practice may be to simply articulate the values that underlie a program and make it effective. Riverside's high-expectations welfare-to-work model, for instance, was one of relatively few programs prior to the mid-1990s that decided it was proper to articulate the value premises that underlay its approach to case management.

OBSERVE THE PRACTICE

In free-lunch-type situations, we can say that the smart practice is "whatever takes advantage of—or exploits—the latent opportunity to create value on the cheap."[6] But let us try to say more about how to characterize this "whatever."

Characterizing the Features of a Smart Practice

The basic mechanism in a smart practice is its means of directly accomplishing useful work in a cost-effective manner. A smart practice is made up of (1) the latent potential for creating value (from Box I-1, p. 10, for instance) plus (2) the mechanism for extracting and focusing that potential. In the six examples described earlier, we indicated the basic mechanisms by saying what each of the practices "takes advantage of." For instance, the shared maintenance for parks takes advantage of potential gains from trade and the opportunity to use barter as a substitute for cash payment.

But there is more to a smart practice than this basic mechanism (Bardach 2004). Some characteristic secondary features of a smart practice are the following:

- *Implementing features*, which directly embody the basic mechanism. In the Oklahoma milestones case, for instance, they are the payment schedule, payment amounts, and payment conditions. In the Hennepin County recycling-rehabilitation program, they are the stock of recyclable materials, the pool of clients with intellectual disabilities, and the interagency understandings that link them.

- *Supportive features*, which are primarily those resources used to bring the implementing features into being—for instance, a budget and an institutional structure. Other supportive features that have a less directly instrumental role but may nevertheless be important might include the culture of the organization or the broader political environment.

- *Optional features*, or those that just happen to be of interest to actors in the site where the practice is observed but may not necessarily be valued elsewhere. For instance, in the Oklahoma milestones case, the feature that allows vendors to participate in the design of the program seems to us optional—although nice!

Distinguishing Functions and Features

Semantic Tip In adapting a seemingly smart practice from a "source site" for application at a "target site," you want to be rigorous in replicating the logic—the *how*—of the basic mechanism, while leaving maximum flexibility as to the specific means to carry it out. To do this, distinguish between the *functions* involved in getting the mechanism to work and the particular *features* that embody those functions. For instance, in the milestones program, the functions include setting the milestones and verifying the claims of achievement. These actions are part of the defining logic of the practice—they cannot be omitted without changing the very essence of the program. However, exactly what features are chosen to implement these functions or to support the implementation strategy is another matter. With regard to the high-expectations welfare-to-work program, two essential functions are creating a moral climate: favoring responsibility and instilling self-confidence that such responsibility can be met. Exactly what design features should be chosen to implement and support these functions is a more open-ended question, though.

Semantic Tip Here is a linguistic hint to help you separate features and functions: Functions should be formulated as gerunds, verb-like nouns ending in "ing"—as in the actions defined earlier as *setting, verifying, creating*, and *instilling*—while the features that perform these functions can be indicated by pure nouns.

An exception to this principle of formulating functional language arises when you really need or want to specify a particular method for carrying out a function. In the milestones case, for instance, you might intentionally refer to a contract as a specific means of defining expectations among the parties and to documents as a means of attesting that the milestones have been met.

Allowing for Variation and Complexity

Because smart practices are internally complex, context sensitive, and capable of being used by different parties to pursue slightly different bundles of goals, how we talk about them should reflect these qualities.

Characterization Should Be Generic and Flexible, Not Prescriptive and Overly Precise. Consider the expenditure control budget described earlier. Does the practice there require giving *all* the savings back to the department, or would, say, 50 percent qualify? If the basic idea is to provide incentives to spend wisely, returning 50 percent may suffice. Probably the best characterization, therefore, would be "allowing the department to retain *enough* of the savings for its staff to feel motivated to create the savings in the first place."[7] It would then be up to whoever implements the expenditure control budget to determine what "enough" means in the local context.

It *should* be left to local implementers to figure out the details of the generic practice that make sense in their own context. Not only does allowing for local adaptation of nonessential features serve common sense, but it encourages as well greater buy-in by the locals to a practice that in some sense is being imported from elsewhere or, worse yet, imposed from outside.

Characterization of the Basic Mechanism of a Smart Practice Is Not Necessarily Simple; It Can Be Complex. Our list of examples of candidate smart practices included only relatively simple practices, so as not to cause confusion. However, some smart practices are multifaceted and thus not easy to summarize in a few sentences or even paragraphs. Michael Barzelay analyzed what he called the "postbureaucratic paradigm" for managing statewide overhead and control functions in Minnesota state government. He considered trying to reduce the many aspects of this postbureaucratic paradigm—which we would also call a smart practice, albeit a very large one—to a few "core ideas" such as service, customer focus, quality, incentives, creating value, and empowerment. However, he concluded, "The major concepts . . . are not organized hierarchically, with one master idea at the top," but are instead arrayed as "an extended family of ideas" (Barzelay 1992, 115–117).

A related management reform paradigm, called by many the "new public management" (NPM), emerged in New Zealand in the mid-1980s as another such extended family of ideas and practices. Noting that it "is not reducible to a few sentences, let alone a slogan," one observer (Borins 1998, 9) goes on to state its key ideas, as follows:

- Government should provide high-quality services that citizens value.

- The autonomy of public managers, particularly from central agency controls, should be increased.

- Organizations and individuals should be evaluated and rewarded on the basis of how well they meet demanding performance targets.

- Managers must be assured that the human and technological resources they need to perform well will be available to them.

- Public-sector managers must appreciate the value of competition and maintain an open-minded attitude about which services belong in the private, rather than the public, sector.

Specimens of a Smart Practice in the Real World Look Rather Different from One Another and Require Careful Interpretation. You should try to find multiple exemplars, or specimens, of a smart practice to get a sense of its robustness and efficacy when (1) it is being implemented under different supportive (or antagonistic) conditions, (2) it comes with different optional features attached, and (3) it employs supposedly equivalent but nevertheless somewhat different means to perform the required functions. Ideally, you would be able to find social scientific evaluation studies of practices that supply both data and theoretical interpretation regarding such matters.

In most cases, however, such evaluations will not exist. Normally—or perhaps at best—you will find writings or speeches by practitioners describing successes in a few places, accompanied by only sketchy descriptions of what was done or the difficulties of implementation. You will need to think very hard and reason very carefully about how you want to conceptualize (that is, define) the smart practice of interest and to assess the support requirements you think are most important. You need to do this even before you get to thinking about how the practice might work in the particular context(s) you have in mind (see the later discussion of this point under "But Will It Work Here?").

DESCRIBE GENERIC VULNERABILITIES

It should be part of standard professional practice in describing smart practices to explain not only how and why they work but also how and why they fail, collapse, backfire, and generally make people sorry they ever tried them. That is, we should be told the nature of their *generic vulnerabilities*. A generic vulnerability is a potential weakness of the practice that is somehow connected with its basic causal structure. It may have to do with a high sensitivity to small errors in execution or with the environment in which the practice is being implemented (e.g., an environment that imposes certain insupportable stresses).

Of course, all political and implementation environments are stressful to a certain degree, and we can reasonably include in the definition of a particular smart practice those features necessary to safeguard it against the more predictable and potentially damaging stresses. Without such safeguards, an otherwise smart practice can become a very dumb practice. For instance, although privatizing certain municipal service functions is a smart practice when would-be private suppliers operate in a competitive market, it might become a very dumb practice under these circumstances: (1) if it were carried out in an environment monopolized by a single supplier, (2) if the bidding process were very corruptible and corrupt interests were to discover this fact, (3) if inappropriate performance measures were stipulated in the contract, or (4) if the municipal contract management procedures were overly rigid or overly lax. To take another example, a high-expectations welfare-to-work program is vulnerable to the condition of the local labor market: If unemployment is high and jobs are scarce, high expectations may produce in participants more defeatism about themselves and more cynicism about the "responsibility" that society is urging on them. A government–neighborhood partnership for park maintenance is, in a generic sense, vulnerable to, among other things, temptations on the part of policymakers to slowly shift more and more of the burden onto the neighbors while reallocating budgetary funds to other departments.

Generic vulnerabilities are only the *potential* for trouble, it should be remembered. Whether the troubles materialize depends on the nature of the local environment in which the smart practice is implemented and on the success of various parties who are aware of the vulnerabilities in designing and implementing successful countermeasures. Contracting processes, for instance, can be designed to minimize corruption, albeit at some cost. And neighbors entering into a partnership with the city regarding parks maintenance can insist on putting the terms of the partnership in writing and holding a well-publicized press conference to announce them. Even if such a document had no legal standing, it might give neighborhood representatives some useful political leverage in later years.

Two particular types of vulnerability are especially worth attending to. One pertains to likely failures of general management capacity—such as a low general level of leadership talent or the lack of a "good government" ethos—that would make it easier to implement this or any other practice successfully. The other pertains to weaknesses intrinsic to the particular practice itself—such as a service delivery program's susceptibility to conflict over whether to give priority to this or that catchment area or needy subpopulation, or a safety-oriented regulatory program's inability to determine whether to err on the side of injury-tolerant leniency or costly stringency.

BUT WILL IT WORK HERE?

Assuming that you have sufficiently understood the essence of the generic smart practice, including its generic vulnerabilities, and have mapped the variety of supportive features that could increase its odds of success, in the end, you must still ask, "Assuming that this practice is indeed smart in some contexts, is ours a context in which it can work well enough to warrant trying it?" Answering this question intelligently entails looking both at the source contexts, where the practice appears to have worked well, and at your own target context, where it is being considered for adoption.

Assessing the Target Context

Within your target context, a careful assessment of the present situation is in order, of course, but a static answer based on this assessment is not enough. You need to think also about what might be done at reasonable cost or risk to improve the prospects of the smart practice in the target context, were it to be implemented there. These actions fall into the following two categories:

- *Safeguarding strategies.* Consider the generic vulnerabilities of the smart practice: Are the most dangerous of them likely to cause unacceptable trouble in your context? For instance, if excessive rigidity in the contract management process is a generic vulnerability of partnering with a nonprofit agency, are your contract management institutions known to be unusually rigid? And if so, is there anything you can do to offset this problem? Might you, for instance, find someone in the contract management bureau who can serve as a special protector and expediter? Or if you cannot do that, can you find some way to structure the contract terms so that the contractor is held accountable for achieving general results rather than for following specific procedures?

- *Enhancement strategies.* Consider what we called earlier the "supportive features" that can help a practice to work better: What supportive features will be put into play? How well are they likely to perform? Can you do anything to improve them? For instance, can you attract top-notch personnel to manage this program or undertake this project? Can you obtain more stable funding than annual appropriations? Can you mobilize the press to take positive notice of what you are doing? Can you count on the support of key stakeholders and relevant political constituencies—or at least on weak action from opponents?

Evaluating the Source Contexts

If you have to search very hard for smart practices that might be usable in your own situation, the chances are that such practices are not widespread. This means that the specimens you locate will come from jurisdictions, agencies, or locales where policymakers and administrators tend to look more favorably on novelty and innovation than is usually the case. Hence, their overall managerial capacity may be better than average—and perhaps better than the one in your own locale.

If the source contexts are largely pilot or demonstration programs, you need to be particularly cautious, because (1) pilot program implementers often bring more enthusiasm and talent to bear on their work than the average program implementers, and enthusiasm and talent count for something; (2) the political and financial conditions at the pilot sites are probably more favorable (or less unfavorable) than those at the average site; and (3) bureaucratic resistance to a pilot program is typically less intense than to a permanent change that threatens existing values, status, job security, or work routines.

How cautious should you be in extrapolating from successes observed in pilot or demonstration contexts? No systematic research exists to answer this question. However, a RAND Corporation analysis of a variety of juvenile crime prevention programs discounted the effectiveness levels attained in the pilot contexts by 15–40 percent when estimating a "scaling up penalty" that would apply when implementing the programs on a wide scale (Greenwood et al. 1995). Although the RAND analysts offered no explicit reasoning for choosing the penalty factors that they did, their choices do seem reasonable.

If you are analyzing the possibility of implementing a smart practice not just in some known local context but on a wide scale, you should be concerned about more than the fact that pilot program results may be much better than average. You should also be concerned about the existence of many *below-average* sites where the smart practice would be implemented—some of them perhaps quite a bit below average. In an era when it was much less common than it is today to think about the federal devolution of program and policy responsibilities to state governments, federal policymakers—particularly political liberals—often worried about the "Mississippi problem." Mississippi was the rhetorical symbol of the poor, backward, and probably racist jurisdiction that would almost surely wreck or pervert any smart practice it was given responsibility for implementing.

BACK TO THE EIGHTFOLD PATH

Given the typical shortfall of good evidence relative to theory and speculation when it comes to assessing a smart practice, there is a danger of unwarranted optimism. Indeed, a common criticism of the best practices research tradition is that it becomes excessively enthusiastic about what appear to be good ideas before their worth is sufficiently tested.[8]

But how much testing is "sufficient," anyway? The answer has to be framed partly in terms of the costs of displacing what might actually be a better practice—perhaps even the practices currently in use (described earlier as "letting present trends continue"). However, if you are reasonably confident that current practices are ineffective or harmful, the costs of wrongly abandoning them in favor of the new and untried may not be so high after all. Thus, although the new and untried should bear *some* burden of proof, it should not be an excessive one. The correct approach is to treat the risks and uncertainties involved in adopting some seemingly smart practice as comparable to the uncertainties associated with all the other alternatives under consideration.

Of course, the costs of change—negotiation, insecurity, hard feelings, and so on—must also be counted against bringing in a new and seemingly smart practice. But such costs must be counted against any change, not just change to accommodate smart practice. Moreover, if institutions and people are very stuck in their ways, there may be benefits to change as such, not merely costs.[9]

NOTES

1. Readers interested in a more social scientific exposition of many of the points in Part IV should consult Bardach (2004).
2. Risks come in several varieties; see the section in Part IV, page 141, titled "Describe Generic Vulnerabilities."

3. This program was a 1997 finalist in the Ford Foundation/Kennedy School of Government (KSG) Innovations in American Government competition. The source for information about it was the Innovations program files.
4. This project was a Ford/KSG semifinalist. See Borins (1998, 200). Note also personal communication (E. Bardach, pers. comm. with Hennepin County program managers).
5. Whether or not contracting out is a smart practice, it is highly controversial, we might add.
6. With minor adjustments, the same analysis can also be applied to practices whose "smartness" derives from their departure from convention.
7. This interpretation is asserted by the researcher-observer; it is not necessarily something that has been done in practice or endorsed by any practitioners.
8. Unfortunately, excessive enthusiasm for experiments that eventually fail gives even appropriate enthusiasm for experimentation a bad name.
9. Alternatively, if institutions and people are forever being reformed and reinvented and remodeled—as occurs in many public school systems—there may be benefits to stability, consistency, and focus.

Appendix A

THINGS GOVERNMENTS DO

The following list of things governments do is meant to stimulate creativity and give you ideas. The way to use it is to think about your policy problem and then go down the list, asking yourself, "Might there be any way to use this approach on this problem?"

The "Why You Might Do It" discussion that accompanies each list of "What You Might Do" is necessarily brief. It is intended principally to be suggestive.

I. TAXES

A. What You Might Do

1. Add a new tax

2. Abolish an old tax

3. Change the tax rate

4. Change the tax base

5. Improve collection machinery

6. Tax an externality

B. Why You Might Do It

The most common conditions to which taxes are a solution are those in which there is inadequate government revenue for some purpose and—probably more important—those in which the structure of market prices fails to capture the true economic opportunity costs. If market prices are wrong, there are usually deeper structural reasons, such as oligopolistic power or government overregulation of some input, which might bear correcting by other means as well.

Naturally, too many taxes can also be a problem, if they are inhibiting useful economic or social activity.

II. REGULATION

A. What You Might Do

1. Add a new regulatory regime or abolish an old one

2. Write new standards or remove old ones

3. Tighten or loosen existing standards

4. Ban or prohibit something entirely

5. Improve the scientific and technical basis for writing standards

6. Close or open loopholes

7. Add, train, or better supervise enforcement personnel

8. Improve targeting of enforcement to catch bad apples, or to increase deterrence, or to increase resource efficiency

9. Raise or lower the level of effective sanctions

10. Tighten or loosen appeals procedures

11. Change reporting and auditing procedures

12. Add, subtract, or improve complaint mechanisms for workers or the public

B. Why You Might Do It

Distinguish three quite different types of regulation. One aims at prices and outputs in natural monopolies—for instance, the historical regulation of local telephone service by a public utilities commission. As this example suggests, technological change (e.g., cell phones, broadband) can undermine natural-monopoly production and render this form of oversight irrelevant.

A second type—sometimes called "social regulation" or "protective regulation" because it seeks to prevent various harms to consumers or workers—is common in regard to health and safety issues. It aims to correct imperfections arising from poor market information or from excessive frictions resulting from the use of civil law (usually tort or contract) remedies. Drug safety regulation by the Food and Drug Administration (FDA) is an example. Bank solvency regulation also fits this category. Two sorts of problems are common in this type of regulation: too little regulation and too much. Scientific uncertainties, technical difficulties of measurement, and political pressures typically lead to both of these problems under varying conditions.

A third type of regulation concerns entry, exit, output, price, and service levels in supposedly oligopolistic industries (e.g., transportation). Administering this type of regulation presents large problems of collecting information and of coordinating the outputs of many firms. Politically, there are often problems of anticompetitive "capture." The deregulation movement that has gathered political momentum since around 1978 has led to a new appreciation of how much beneficial competition there might be in these industries if government were simply to let go.

Most air and water pollution regulation is thought of as social regulation. However, administratively (and sometimes politically), it is more like the third type of regulation, inasmuch as the principal laws now on the books involve government agencies in coordinating the outputs of a variety of firms.

III. SUBSIDIES AND GRANTS

A. What You Might Do

1. Add a new one

2. Abolish an old one

3. Change the level

4. Change the marginal rate

5. Introduce, abolish, or change a formula by which subsidies are allocated

6. Modify the conditions of receipt or eligibility

7. Loosen enforcement

8. Tighten enforcement

B. Why You Might Do It

Incentive Effects. Subsidies and grants are often used to stimulate activities that neither markets nor nonprofit or voluntary action appears to produce in adequate quantity or quality. They also play important roles in the system of intergovernmental relationships—when one level of government wishes to encourage another level of government to do certain things—and in the system of relationships between governments and nonprofit organizations.

Wealth Effects. Grants and subsidies also transfer resources to people or organizations or levels of government in order to make the recipients wealthier.

Some Design Problems. It often happens that you want to create incentive effects but not wealth effects, or vice versa. For instance, you may wish to make poor people wealthier via grants and subsidies but without diminishing work incentives. Or you may wish to encourage businesses or universities to undertake more research and development of a certain kind but without unduly enriching them or allowing them to use the subsidies inefficiently.

Note that subsidies and grants are typically administered with various guidelines or conditions attached. The threat to remove a longtime grant or subsidy for violation of the guidelines or conditions can act as a type of regulatory sanction, thus making certain grants and subsidies into a peculiar regulatory hybrid.

IV. SERVICE PROVISION

A. What You Might Do

1. Add a new service

2. Expand an existing service

3. Organize outreach to potential beneficiaries not now using the service

4. Better customize an existing service to a particular subpopulation

5. Provide vouchers for a particular service so that people may choose from an array of competitive service providers

6. Link two or more existing service delivery systems to take advantage of potential synergies or to make life easier for service recipients

7. Reduce service users' difficulties in accessing the service by
    a. going online
    b. computerizing intake and eligibility processes
    c. simplifying forms
    d. colocating services
    e. permitting appointments by phone
    f. facilitating personal inquiries and complaints
    g. improving payment options

B. Why You Might Do It

Services come in two basic flavors. *Desired services* are those that people want, such as parks and good schools. *Paternalistic services* are those that people may or may not want but that outsiders want them to have because there is some potential payoff to the outsiders (e.g., rehabilitative services for the mentally ill, organized shelters for the homeless, job search services for individuals on welfare). It is a lot easier to design a service provision system for desired services than to do so for paternalistic services.

V. AGENCY BUDGETS

A. What You Might Do

1. Add a lot to the budget

2. Add just a little to the budget

3. Hold the budget at last year's level

4. Cut the budget a little

5. Cut the budget a lot—to the point of beginning to terminate the agency

6. Shift allocations from one budget item to another

B. Why You Might Do It

You may want to adjust an agency's budget according to whether you like what it does. In addition, how you manipulate an agency's budget sends political signals about the degree of satisfaction or dissatisfaction with the agency's performance and so may be thought to have incentive effects as well as wealth effects. It is not easy to use the budget as a means of creating incentive effects, however.

VI. INFORMATION

A. What You Might Do

1. Require disclosure

2. Direct government rating or certification

3. Standardize display or format

4. Simplify information

5. Subsidize production of information

6. Subsidize dissemination of information

B. Why You Might Do It

Information production, dissemination, and validation may be suboptimal due to the declining average (and sometimes marginal) cost nature of the activity. Information consumption may be suboptimal due to the hidden costs of consumption (such as time spent reading or hearing or interpreting or sifting or verifying).

VII. THE STRUCTURE OF PRIVATE RIGHTS

A. What You Might Modify or Create

1. Contract rights and duties

2. Property rights

3. Liability duties

4. Family law

5. Constitutional rights

6. Labor law

7. Corporate law

8. Criminal law

9. Dispute-resolving institutions other than litigation and courts

B. Why You Might Do It

In recent years, two of the biggest issues drawing the attention of policy analysts and economists interested in legal institutions have been the economically efficient incidence of risk—it should fall on the party that can manage it at the lowest social cost—and the costs involved in administering any adjudicative system. Since private-law duties and rights do a lot to allocate risk (e.g., if your product exposes the user to risk and ultimately injury, you may be liable for damages, unless perhaps the user abused or misused it or agreed to assume the risks of use), adjusting laws is sometimes a powerful policy intervention mechanism. Also, much creative thinking has gone into finding ways to reduce the administrative and adjudicative costs.

In addition to these economic matters, there is concern about compensation for harm. Laws can be changed so as to shift wealth—in some prospective, actuarial sense or in a real, present-time sense—among different interests or classes of people.

The wealth-shifting and risk-shifting effects of legal changes may both work in the desired direction, or they may work at cross-purposes. In addition, both may work together with, or at cross-purposes with, the desire to reduce administrative and adjudicative costs.

VIII. THE FRAMEWORK OF ECONOMIC ACTIVITY

A. What You Might Do

1. Encourage competition

2. Encourage concentration

3. Control prices and wages (and profits)

4. Decontrol prices and wages (and profits)

5. Control output levels

6. Decontrol output levels

7. Change tax incentives up or down

8. Provide public jobs

9. Abolish public jobs

B. Why You Might Do It

Supporting More Governmental Intervention. On the supply side, there may be monopoly or oligopoly problems. On the demand side, consumers may be relatively nonmobile or otherwise vulnerable to exploitation—and the same may be true of workers.

Supporting Less Governmental Intervention. You may decide that political forces have captured the government administrative apparatus and perverted the intent, or that the information costs to government entailed in doing the job well are simply too high, or that technology has changed and made an older form of governmental intervention less appropriate or effective or efficient.

IX. EDUCATION AND CONSULTATION

A. What You Might Do

1. Warn of hazards or dangers

2. Raise consciousness through exhortation or inspiration

3. Provide technical assistance

4. Upgrade skills and competencies

5. Change values

6. Professionalize the providers of a service through training or certification or licensing

B. Why You Might Do It

People may be unaware of a problem or an opportunity. They may be careless or unfeeling. There may be too many untrained or unskilled people in jobs demanding too much responsibility.

X. FINANCING AND CONTRACTING

A. What You Might Do

1. Create a new (governmental) market

2. Abolish an existing (governmental) market

3. Alter reimbursement rates

4. Change the basis for reimbursement (e.g., cost-plus, price per unit, sliding scale dependent on quantity, performance bonuses or penalties)

5. Lease governmentally held resources

6. Alter user fee structure

7. Redesign bidding systems

8. Change contract enforcement methods

9. Furnish loans

10. Guarantee loans

11. Subsidize loans

12. Set up a public enterprise

13. Dismantle a public enterprise

14. "Privatize" a hitherto public enterprise

15. Modify insurance arrangements

16. Change procurement practices

B. Why You Might Do It

Capital and/or insurance markets may be working inefficiently. The governmental contracting and procurement machinery may not be operating well—it may be too rigid, or too corrupt, or too expensive, or too slow.

XI. BUREAUCRATIC AND POLITICAL REFORMS

A. What You Might Do

The number of possibilities is too great to list. It ranges across such activities as reorganizations, replacing top supervisory personnel, improving information systems, and raising wages and salaries.

B. Why You Might Do It

The substantive reasons are too numerous to list. We should note, though, that in many policy contexts, there are important political and symbolic considerations for undertaking bureaucratic and political reforms. The political considerations often involve enhancing the power of one social interest or point of view at the expense of another. The symbolic considerations often involve ducking the really hard or impossible problems at the social level in favor of doing something readily seen in a domain over which government appears to have control (that is, its own operations).

Appendix B

UNDERSTANDING PUBLIC AND NONPROFIT INSTITUTIONS

Asking the Right Questions

Policy analysis, properly done, requires you to think not only about the technical aspects of governmental action but also about its institutional aspects—that is, the institutions that implement policy. Whether implementation goes well or poorly depends in part on whether the relevant institutions want to facilitate or impede the policy at hand. But motivation is not the whole story; capacity is at least as important. Here we want to draw attention primarily to the aspects of organizational structure and process that bear on capacity, and we do so not by offering a detailed exposition but by posing some (forty-one) questions that the analyst ought to be asking.

MISSION

1: What is the mission of the agency?
   - As expressed in authoritative sources?
   - As understood and enacted by agency managers and employees?

ENVIRONMENT

2: What support/opposition does the agency have for its mission, and for itself, in its "authorizing environment"—that is, the totality of actors whose legal and nonlegal attitudes and actions determine agency legitimacy in the polity?
   - Evidence from budgetary allocations?
   - Other evidence?

3: Is the task environment relatively placid, changing predictably, or changing unpredictably? Examples follow of what is meant by these terms:
   - *Placid:* telephone company in 1975
   - *Changing predictably:* hospitals in the 1970s, before managed care but in the era when changing technologies were introduced and when overcapacity was looming

- *Changing unpredictably:* telecommunications companies today; hospitals today, facing changes in the insurance marketplace, in technology, and in government policies

Note that the less predictability and the faster the pace of change, the greater the need for getting information from the organization's field people rapidly, allowing them to make at least some decisions on their own, and making grand strategic shifts from the center.

4: Who are the agency's main competitors for resources and/or domain of legitimate action?

5: Does the agency have a comparative advantage—or disadvantage—in meeting the competition?

6: Does the agency face rivals who don't merely compete with but are downright hostile to aspects of the agency's mission or philosophy?

PERFORMANCE MEASUREMENT

7: What metrics are available to tell us how effectively and efficiently the agency is performing?
- Producing outputs and outcomes?

    Outputs are what you can operationally count as a result of the agency's productive work, such as number of students graduated, number of acres of forest thinned, or number of passengers carried per day. *Outcomes* are consequences of the outputs that we actually value per se, such as greater employability of those students, greater fire resistance of those forests, reduction in transportation time or in pollution levels, or increases in transportation satisfaction.

    It is usually (much) harder to measure outcomes than outputs.

    Outcomes are the product of more than the agency's outputs. Hence, crediting or blaming the agency for the quality of the outcomes is not straightforward.

8: Agency quality is compared to what benchmarks or standards?
- Other similar organizations?
- The same agency in previous years?
- An absolute standard?

9: What additional metrics would you, ideally, like to see?

10: Who are the agency's "customers," if any? Are they being well served? What is their opinion?

- It is easy to see a park user as a customer of the parks department.

- But is a taxpayer a customer of the Internal Revenue Service (IRS)?

- Is the student a customer of the school? Or is her family?

TECHNOLOGY

Technology is a slightly fuzzy word, more easily defined by example than by abstractions.

11: To what extent does the agency use a service-delivery technology? A regulatory technology? A people-changing technology? A project technology?

- *Service-delivery technology:* a transportation agency's provision of vehicles and other facilities for use by patrons, writing and mailing Social Security checks, and issuance of annual auto registration plates or stickers

- *Regulatory technology:* command-and-control activities, such as environmental inspection and enforcement; Occupational Safety and Health Administration (OSHA) regulations; and restaurant sanitation inspections

- *People-changing technology:* education, probation, and child protective services

- *Project technology:* issuance of a land-use plan, construction of a convention center, and immunization of all youngsters against this year's strain of flu

12: Is it a strong or a weak technology?

- A *strong technology*—such as writing Social Security checks—is replicable and works in all contexts.

- A *weak technology*—such as counseling probationers—is not easily replicated and is sensitive to social context and individual-level competency.

    The structure and process you use to run an agency will depend to some degree on the type of technology you are implementing, partly for technical reasons and partly for political reasons: you get into trouble if you adopt a regulatory attitude when you should be serving a customer, and vice versa.

13: Is the agency's authority structure appropriate to the agency's mission, technology, and human resources?

14: Is the agency's internal division of labor appropriate to the agency's mission, technology, and human resources?

15: Does the agency have effective means—formal and/or informal—to create working relationships across unit boundaries?

PRODUCTION/DELIVERY PROCESSES

16: What is (are) the principal process(es) the organization uses to implement its production technology(ies)—that is, to produce its outputs?

> This question is complicated because it focuses on processes that connect the organization's activities, the human and physical materials it works on, and the way in which it transforms materials.

- In environmental and other kinds of command-and-control regulation, we have processes of standard setting, inspections for compliance with standards, and the threat and actuality of punishment for noncompliance, a complicated form of deterrence.

- In a welfare program, the process involves determinations of eligibility and amount.

FRONTLINE WORKERS AND CO-PRODUCERS

17: Are the frontline workers doing a good job? Are they competent? Motivated? Adequately supported by the organization?

18: What systems of incentives, supervision, and support are in place to motivate them, help them, and hold them accountable? Are the means of recruiting them suited to getting individuals with the right qualifications?

19: Does the organization make full use of the talents and information residing at the frontline level?

20: To what extent does the agency also rely on "co-producers"—people and organizations that share in the production process without being employed by the agency?

- Welfare recipients are co-producers, along with the welfare agency, to the extent that they assist, and are assisted by, the agency in their efforts to find jobs.
- Parents co-produce their children's education along with the children's teachers.
- Along with the environmental regulatory agency, complying firms co-produce environmental improvement.

21: Does the agency manage its co-producers well? Does it provide the proper tools? Information? Motivation?

PARTNERS AND OTHER OUTSIDERS

22: To what extent does the agency rely on public and not-for-profit partners to accomplish its mission? Does it manage these relationships effectively?[1]

23: Does the agency rely heavily on for-profit vendors? Does it manage these relationships effectively?

24: Does the agency effectively manage its relationships with governmental "overhead" (or "control" or "staff") agencies—such as the Departments of Finance or Budget, Personnel, Procurement, Audit, and so on?

CENTRALIZATION/DECENTRALIZATION

25: If the organization delivers services at multiple sites (as in a school district), does it have an effective balance of centralization and decentralization?

26: Does it use its internal budget-making procedures to structure incentives for performance improvements and cost reductions?

CULTURE AND COMMUNICATIONS

27: Does the agency have a relatively "strong" or "weak" culture?

- *Strong culture:* the US Navy, the local fire department, the US Forest Service, the California Legislative Analyst's Office

- *Weak culture:* many contemporary public health departments, many inner-city public schools

28: Is the culture relatively hierarchical or egalitarian? Rules oriented or performance oriented, or both? Where do efficiency and cost minimization fit in?

29: Are communications within the agency relatively unconstrained by hierarchy and/or by subunit boundaries? Are people relatively unafraid to speak their minds, or are they circumspect and cautious? Is entrepreneurship encouraged or discouraged?

30: Do senior managers attempt to "lead through culture"? How?

31: Are creativity and innovation valued within the agency? Does the agency make systematic efforts to stimulate creativity and innovation?

POLITICS

32: Are there factions within the organization? If so, are they based on professional, ideological, or bureaucratic cleavages? On other factors?

33: Does factional competition or conflict degrade organizational performance or—by stimulating effort and healthy competition—improve it?

34: How do senior managers deal with the existence of factions?

LEADERSHIP

35: Who, if anyone, is a leader in this organization?

36: How does such a person gain and preserve legitimacy?

37: How effective is (are) the leader(s)?

38: What functions do they play in the organization?

39: What strategies do they use to carry out their leadership functions?

CHANGE

40: Is there a culture of *continuous improvement*—a term originally associated with the Total Quality Management (TQM) movement—and learning from mistakes?

41: Does the agency have the capacity and motivation to scan the environment for signs of opportunity or danger? If such signs are present, can the agency adapt effectively?

NOTE

1. For an extensive discussion, see Bardach (1998).

Appendix C

STRATEGIC ADVICE ON THE DYNAMICS OF GATHERING POLITICAL SUPPORT

This *Practical Guide* is largely about the intellectual aspects of policy analysis done in the public interest. Its lofty focus should not obscure the fact that the adoption of policy occurs through a process that is often untainted by much intellectuality at all and is subject to the pushing and hauling of various stakeholders, many of them more concerned about holding power, winning elections, and aiding their "side" than about promoting "the public interest."

All policy is political, whether the politics takes place in a back room or within a legislature, an organization, or a community. You must build support and neutralize opponents. To do this, at the interpersonal level, you must make arguments, frame and reframe "the facts," call in favors, and imply threats. At the organizational and institutional levels, you must mobilize allies; manipulate arenas, calendars, and procedural rules; offer (and extract) concessions; and negotiate side payments.

All these issues of attitude and influence involve a good deal of calculation and estimation: Which agency's budget will grow larger or smaller; whose turf will be expanded or diminished? How much weight, or influence, do these supporting and opposing interests carry with the key decision-makers anyway? We ignore all such questions here, although in your work you must both ask them and develop the information to answer them. The elementary answers are fairly obvious, however, and the sophisticated answers would take up too much space. (Example question: Will agencies support policies that expand their budgets and powers? Elementary answer: Yes. Sophisticated answer: Usually yes, but probably not if such expansion risks changing internal power relations drastically or exposing the agency to possible failure and criticism, etc. Even more sophisticated answer: . . . [This we leave to your imagination and experience.])

One might say that these matters of attitude and influence are instances of *static* analysis, meaning an analysis that assumes the resources of the players are fixed, and that the outcome of a conflict over a proposal doesn't turn on when (or the order in which) each side moves. Journalists' and political scientists' accounts of the policy process are rich in such instances. Static analysis is a reasonable starting place for your assessment of the political feasibility of the alternatives under consideration. But you should not stop there. You should also consider a *dynamic* analysis of the process, which involves questions of sequence (what you should do before, or after, you do some other thing in order to increase your probability of success) and timing (what to do "early" or "late" in the projected course of a months- or possibly years-long campaign to build "enough" support).[1]

The assumption here is that one can make a list of generic "things to do," based on general knowledge of how such efforts on behalf of policy proposals play themselves out; then, postulate a generic flow of threats and opportunities over the course of such a campaign; and, finally, map the list of things to do into this flow with the object of realizing a high likelihood of winning. More precisely, you want to do the mapping not only with winning in mind but also with the idea of conserving political and other resources so that they will be available for other campaigns.

As a basic example, let us consider the case of a political entrepreneur—an actor who tries to "sell" a novel policy proposal to stakeholders, not merely respond to existing preferences—trying to get a bill passed by a legislative body. The general outline of the process and of entrepreneurial strategy should apply to roughly analogous situations as well, such as trying to win approval from senior management to try some organizational innovation.

Start with the idea that you need to accumulate *Support*[2] from a variety of *Interests* (construed very broadly, and including individuals as well as groups or organizations) up to the point that you have *Enough Support* to swing the balance toward legislative victory for some *Proposal*. For the sake of concreteness, think about passing a bill to remove an existing statute requiring mandatory minimum sentences for drug users and low-level dealers, while retaining them for high-level dealers. (For an excellent policy analysis of this idea, see the RAND report "Mandatory Minimum Drug Sentences: Throwing Away the Key or the Taxpayers' Money?" available at www.rand.org/pubs/monograph_reports/MR827.html.)

Assume that there is a hazily perceived and somewhat movable *End Date*, months or years off and linked to *Allies*'[3] willingness to plug along before concluding that the cause is lost and that other drug policy issues now deserve their attention and other *Resources*. The basic rule is this: If your Proposal accumulates Enough Support at the moment of the End Date, you win; otherwise you lose. What sequencing and timing strategies and tactics should you deploy?

SEQUENCING

First, consider the problem of sequencing, in particular whether getting some Interests on board first will make it politically easier to approach others subsequently. Who might these primary Interests be?

- Persons with drug-policy expertise who agree with your conclusion that mandatory minimum sentences are appropriate only for high-level dealers, as well as persons or groups with a reputation for soundness, judgment, and ideological compatibility, might clear the way for Interests concerned about the practicality and efficacy of your Proposal.

- For Interests with an internal hierarchy, such as a state substance abuse agency or a political party organization, getting Support from experts or influentials lower down might require getting clearance from individuals higher up in the hierarchy.

- Access to particularly *Weighty* individuals, such as the chair of the Assembly Committee on Criminal Justice, might require working through a chain of introductions and connections. Note that "weight" is determined not only by actors' access to formal authority but also by their political reputation and standing (e.g., the support of an actor normally expected to oppose your proposal—such as an actor who has opposed similar measures in the past or who belongs to an organization or party known to favor tough antidrug legislation in this example) might be especially "weighty" and alter perceptions of the viability of your idea.

TIMING

One aspect of timing involves trying to stimulate bandwagon effects: Get some Weighty Interests on board early in order to create the impression that success is inevitable, which will (1) draw in Interests concerned primarily with being on the winning side and (2) *Neutralize*, at least for the time being, Interests who might otherwise go into active opposition.

Other aspects of timing are more subtle. Suppose that you have a rough but generally reliable time profile (or map) of *Opportunities* and threats that tend to emerge relatively early or relatively late in the course of a campaign. You are thus able to time your actions so as to capitalize on the Opportunities and Neutralize the threats. You are also able to (roughly) plan to expend certain Resources early in order to capitalize on the Opportunities that come early on and then vanish forever, and to conserve certain *(Depletable) Resources* for the threats that you can anticipate toward the middle and end of the process.[4] And, if you are lucky, you may never have to expend those Resources at all.

For instance, early in the campaign you want to win over those Interests who will be enthusiastic Supporters and active recruiters—that is, real Allies. They will help you with raising money and gaining access to other such tangible Resources as office space, talented staffers, strategic advisers, and communications experts.

Unfortunately for you, repealing mandatory minimum sentences is not a policy Proposal that engages a natural constituency of Resource-rich potential Allies. You might find a few drug-policy and criminal-justice policy experts, some grassroots ethnic advocacy groups (who observe that their ethnic confreres are disproportionately locked up under the current laws), possibly the state university system (which sees scarce budget dollars diverted from higher education to build more prisons for ever-growing populations of prisoners), and perhaps the odd taxpayer group concerned with the budget and the tax burden more generally. But, whatever the limitations of their endowments, these are the sorts of Allies with *Marketing Resources* that you will need to go into business. In fact, you need them so much in the early days of the campaign that you will need to expend cash, call in political *Debts*, and ask for political *Favors* (that is, go into Debt yourself).

These early days represent a significant Opportunity for utilization of your scarce Resources for one very important reason: the *Opposition* will not yet have mobilized. (The Opposition is likely to include, among others, politicians who find support for "law and order" a useful electoral tool; contractors and subcontractors who profit from the prison-building boom; rural communities for whom prisons are a valuable source of employment; and the prison guards union.) You and your Allies will be able to hold the stage yourselves, make your pitch—that is, "Tell Your Story"—and hype the bandwagon aspects of your coalition's progress.

Why is the Opposition silent? It takes time for its members to organize themselves, and some may be temporarily occupied with more pressing matters anyway. Most important, they know that most such attempts at significant policy change simply die of their own accord, and so they may not need to go out of their way to kill this one. Indifference, skepticism, the comfort of the known, and the veto-enabling character of our political institutions (e.g., checks and balances) pose a high barrier to change. Although these Opposition skeptics are right, they nevertheless are giving you a brief moment in the sun, which you would be wise to seize, even if it means taking certain risks.

As the Support for your Proposal visibly rises, however, the Opposition manages to organize a countermobilization. (All proposals—even socially beneficial ideas—entail trade-offs, and it is usually not too hard for opponents to find some concern to rally around.) Let us assume this countermobilization succeeds in stalling your efforts to persuade Interests that are still uncommitted and even manages to Neutralize a few of the Interests you thought you had won to your cause.

Now is the time to expend some of the Depletable Resources[5] you have been conserving and perhaps to borrow a little against the future as well. What are these Resources?

- First, Debts—owed to you (and your coalition Allies) in exchange for past Favors you have done the indebted parties—that you can now call in.

- Second, policy *Concessions* you can make—that is, amendments to your Proposal. In this case, you might offer to enlarge the definition of "high-level dealer" beyond what you had originally proposed.

- Third, normative expectations about the contributions of Allies that you can implicitly enforce—for instance, "As we are all in this together, it would be helpful if one of your people could make a call on Representative X."

- Finally, Debts that you can create (up to some limit, of course, which is why this is a Depletable Resource) by asking Favors.

But note well: Although expending all such Resources is costly, Concessions may be doubly costly, because a Concession on policy usually represents either a goal or an objective foregone and also, possibly, a seeming breach of loyalty with Allies who have already signed on in the hopes of passing the very element of the Proposal that you are giving up. (Perhaps the ethnic advocacy Interests who signed on early will be severely alienated by your enlargement of the pool of "high-level dealers.") Hence, in this recovery phase, you stand a very good chance of raising fears among all your Allies that their hearts' desires are also in jeopardy.

Given that you can anticipate these coalition-fragmenting developments, you can take one or more prophylactic measures: build in potential Concessions (bargaining chips) of relatively low value to you and your Allies early in the contest—such as starting with an extremely restricted definition of high-level dealers—so that they may be ceded during the recovery phase; accumulate a surplus of Allies and Supporters as a buffer against defections by the angry and disappointed during the recovery phase; and develop a reputation for integrity that can withstand suspicions of carelessness and disloyalty.

At some point, the Proposal is embodied in a bill, and the contest over the bill gets structured by the procedures of the legislature—its committees, its rules, and its calendars. The *Attentive Public* expands as well. Earlier, it had included mostly Interests concerned about the policies and Resources pertaining to drugs and criminal justice. Now it includes legislators (and staff) who are concerned about the Proposal's possible uses in partisan, institutional, and interpersonal competition. The relevance of Marketing Resources declines relative to that of more political Resources, which can be brought to bear on the manipulation of legislative procedures and the augmentation of Support or the Neutralizing of Opposition by the use of *Side Payments*. Neutralization is especially useful—for instance, promising to support the prison guards' union in its next bid for a wage increase.

Also, as the contest approaches its increasingly less obscure End Date, and the margin of possible victory or defeat becomes thinner and clearer (in contests destined to be close), both Allies and Opponents engage in riskier maneuvers in regard to an increasingly heterogeneous and volatile Attentive Public, with somewhat unpredictable effects. In this *End Game* phase of high risk and uncertainty, you want to have a goodly store of highly *Fungible Resources*, such as callable Debts and *Goodwill*, which also happen to be Depletable. Hence, it is prudent to conserve these more political and Fungible Resources until this time, even though they might have been of some use in earlier phases as well. To put it epigrammatically, if the speaker of the assembly owes you a Favor, it's the ace of trumps, and don't play it until you absolutely need to.

The process of gathering political support is sensitive to the unfolding of threats and opportunities as the contest goes on. This "unfolding" is in a general sense predictable, although with respect to specifics, it is not. It is full of surprises. We have tried to convey the nature of this unfolding process, through words, with the aim of helping you anticipate and then adapt to such surprises. But it is likely that a more systematic and quantitative approach to this unfolding process would be even more helpful. Computational modeling furnishes such an approach. With a colleague, Professor David Wheat at the University of Bergen, Norway, we are trying to develop such models, using as a platform the System Dynamics tools originally developed in the early 1960s by Jay Forrester at the Massachusetts Institute of Technology. Readers interested in these efforts can learn about them on a related website:

www.wheatresources.com/models/Policy Dynamics.zip

NOTES

1. For a more elaborate discussion of dynamic analysis in general, see Bardach (2006); and see also a very early effort, Bardach (1972). For an effort to describe the dynamics of building an interagency collaborative, see Bardach (2008).
2. From here on, we capitalize terms—and italicize them on first occurrence—that could be integrated into a formal model and, in that context, would deserve precise definition. There are relatively few such terms, and they would make an economical but, we believe, powerful model. For our purposes here, however, the context and the everyday meanings of the terms make the concepts clear enough.

3. Allies are Supporters who are also active in trying to woo potential new Supporters and in attempting to Neutralize actual or potential Opponents.
4. As a logical matter, you would also be able to plan to Neutralize any threats that emerged early and seize Opportunities that emerged late. But as an empirical matter, we do not think these possibilities important enough to discuss here.
5. A Depletable Resource is one that, when used, is used up. Examples are money and Debts that are called in. Requests for Favors establish future liabilities; and the capacity for honoring them is in some sense Depletable, the exceptional case being that of reinvestment of Favors in such a way that overall capacity is augmented, much as business loans can lead to larger profits and even more successful enterprise.

Appendix D

TIPS FOR WORKING WITH CLIENTS

The ideal client

- Gives you a well-defined problem

- Keeps an open mind about the possible solutions

- Yearns to understand its magnitude and its probable future trajectory

- Puzzles over why the problem exists

- Welcomes evidence bearing on the likely effectiveness of various possible alternatives to dealing with it

- Bravely faces up to the necessity for trade-offs in choosing among possible alternatives

- Helps you get access—and in a timely manner—to whatever data sources you need, including statistical information, archival materials, and personal interviews

- Gives you timely feedback on your interim products and advice about fruitful next moves

- Respects the constraints you have on your time, both professional and personal

- Refrains from making ill-considered requests for information or mini-analyses that—in your opinion—will not contribute to the product you both desire

- Accords you appropriate credit among your peers and other audiences for the fine work you have been doing (and with such diligence too!)

- Stands foursquare by your side when your work is unjustly criticized for crass political reasons

The ideal client exists—but you are probably not working for him or her. Assuming this is so, how can you deal with the problems that might arise in the relationship?

Many of the answers would take us into the more general realm of human and professional relationships, and we will not presume to advise on these. We will focus only on problems that are particular to the analyst–client relationship. We touch on just five of the more common ones, and provide tips that are merely suggestive and in any case need to be tailored to the particulars of the situation.

But first two words of caution: tread softly. You could very well turn out to be wrong. Very likely the client understands many things that you do not. Respect for the client is in order, not to say humility.

1. *Problem:* The client's organization turns out to be more a part of the problem than a part of the solution.

   a. *Tip:* You might need to abandon a first-best alternative that draws attention to this in favor of an acceptable second-best alternative. If this is not possible or desirable, imagine yourself in the role of senior official of the client organization and think through (1) ways to mitigate the damage that might be done by publicly embracing the first-best alternative and (2) political and public relations strategies that build up the creditable imagery of the organization. Also, think through ways for your immediate client to survive being the bearer of bad news to other people in the organization.

2. *Problem:* The client organization and/or your liaison has a "pet solution" to your policy problem, which you are more and more convinced is a bad idea.

   a. *Tip:* See if you can avoid being the bearer of the bad news yourself. Perhaps somebody else will do it? If not, see if you can develop a process through which the client organization can come to see for itself that its pet solution is a bad idea.

3. *Problem:* You find that the original definition of "the problem" as presented to you by the client organization is misleading and should best be changed to one that makes much more sense to you.

   a. *Tip:* Do most of your work using your substitute problem definition, but treat it as an addition to your project when talking to the client, not as a substitute. Do what you can, within reason, to satisfy the client's needs or desires with respect to the original problem definition. Over time, develop a process whereby the client organization comes to see for itself that your work within your new framework is more to the point than sticking to the old framework.

4. *Problem:* The person within the client organization who had been your original and ongoing liaison leaves the organization and is replaced by someone unfamiliar with your work and not too interested in it.

   a. *Tip:* Sit down with the liaison and ask him or her to advise you. If the liaison person has hitherto not thought much about the transition problem, or has not shown much interest in helping you solve it, spend a minute up front underlining the main difficulties you foresee. Make the point that the liaison probably has potentially better insight into the situation than anyone else, including yourself.

   b. *Tip:* Develop good relations with other individuals within the organization, so that you will not be completely stranded should your liaison disappear. As well as being a good precautionary strategy, this will help when it comes time to market your work.

5. *Problem:* Your analytical project has low priority in the mind of the liaison, who is busy with more important, more pressing matters.

   a. *Tip:* Consider: If one takes the broad view, perhaps your client has the right priorities and you are being too self-centered about your needs. But if you conclude that your view of appropriate priorities is more right than your client's, try to understand better what your client's priorities really are and, to the extent possible, put a "spin" on your work so that it can be seen to fit better with them.

Appendix E

SUGGESTIONS FOR INCORPORATING "BIG DATA" AND RIGOROUS SCIENTIFIC EVIDENCE INTO POLICY ANALYSIS

Two of the most significant trends in the field of policy analysis are (1) the growing use of randomized controlled trials (RCTs) and "quasi-experimental methods" such as instrumental variable (IV), regression discontinuity (RD), and difference-in-differences (DD) techniques to generate rigorous scientific evidence on the causal impact of policy interventions and (2) the increasing use of large, digitized administrative data sets (a type of "Big Data"). These trends have been encouraged by the creation of "policy labs" such as The Lab @ DC, the Abdul Latif Jameel Poverty Action Lab (J-PAL), and the California Policy Lab, which work closely with governments to evaluate public programs and inform future decisions.

A full understanding of "Big Data" and experimentation gets into the realm of "machine learning," the logic of causal identification, and privacy protection. These matters are outside the scope of this book.

Here we simply wish to provide a few tips to analysts who are not computer scientists or PhD-level data researchers but who seek to incorporate "evidence-based policy" into their work.

WHERE TO BEGIN

1. If you have at least eight weeks to work on a problem and have a plausible policy solution to test, you might explore whether a policy lab could design and evaluate a pilot intervention. While RCTs are not always feasible, you may be surprised at how easy it is for a policy lab to perform a quick-cycle experiment.

2. If your time is constrained, you can still consult registries of RCTs and other rigorous studies as part of the "Assemble Some Evidence" step to see if a policy similar to your proposal has been evaluated in the past. See J-PAL's database at www.povertyactionlab.org/evaluations.

3. Be sure to learn about the contexts in which impact evaluations of other programs were performed. Investigate whether and how these contexts differ from the context in which your proposal would be implemented.

4. Even if another program, shown to achieve desirable outcomes through a rigorous impact study, was carried out in a context different from your own, you may still decide that the program holds enough promise to test it in your context. See the discussion of "But Will It Work Here?" in Part IV.

5. Remember the opportunity cost of obtaining rigorous evidence. The value of the additional evidence equals the value of the outcome you would get from a decision with better evidence minus the value of the outcome you'd get from a decision without it.

KNOW YOUR DATA

1. It is always important for policy analysts to understand the data they are working with, but this is especially so when you are working with an administrative data set that includes hundreds of thousands or even millions of observations. It is easy to mistake data quantity for data quality.

2. Data cleaning is an important task in the use of administrative data sets, and (even if you do not perform the cleaning yourself) you should know how missing, corrupt, or inaccurate records were identified and corrected.

3. Characteristics of "good" administrative data sets include official data of record that are comprehensive with respect to the relevant populations and are often sensitive and hard to get. Characteristics of "bad" administrative data are selectiveness (lack of denominator data), too little information about demographics, and excessive complexities of linkage and privacy issues.[1]

4. It is becoming increasingly easy to query old data sets. Consider whether administrative data collected in the past (e.g., student outcomes from a long ago remedial education program similar to the one you are considering now) could shed light on your questions.

5. Do not denigrate the value of descriptive data—just getting a statistical handle on a massive population can be helpful for many policy analysis tasks. Your guesses about the demographic profile of people enrolled in a social program, or the incomes of homeowners who owe back property taxes, for instance, could turn out to be wide of the mark.

6. Using administrative data is not a substitute for qualitative analysis. Indeed, leading data-driven policy researchers report they gain the most insight when they pair administrative data with detailed knowledge of institutions and programs.[2]

USE ADMINISTRATIVE DATA AND EXPERIMENTS TO INFORM PROBLEM DEFINITION

1. While large administrative data sets are clearly a useful resource for assembling evidence, they can assist your work on other steps of the Eightfold Path as well.

2. "Big Data" can inform problem definition by allowing the analyst to get a quick sense of what is happening on the ground. What high schools in the state have seen the largest increases in their dropout rates over the past decade? How many children currently enrolled in the state's Medicaid program have a parent who is unemployed or was unemployed in the past year? How many of these children are also enrolled in a free lunch program? How many people were served by each of the state's hospital emergency rooms last year, and what demographic, health, insurance status, or other factors correlate with high levels of emergency room use? Even simple cross-tabs generated through large data sets can sometimes provide insights.

3. Experiments can help you evaluate the causal chain that goes from situations to bad effects. You may learn through an experiment whether low income lowers health, whether poor health leads to lower income, or if the causal arrow between income and health points in both directions in a given population.

EXPAND YOUR OPTION SET AND SEE CONSTRAINTS AS LEARNING OPPORTUNITIES

1. Machine learning and other methods can pinpoint factors associated with policy outcomes of interest. This can help you expand your menu of policy alternatives by identifying *potentially* low-hanging fruit—low-cost changes that might (although this would have to be confirmed through more rigorous studies) make a big difference.

2. Learn to see programmatic constraints as learning opportunities. For example, if all eligible persons cannot be enrolled in a program due to

budget limits, consider randomizing access to the program to permit rigorous evaluation of its impact. (Randomizing access from a wait list may also have the advantage of being a more equitable rationing mechanism than "first come, first served.")

USE DATA VISUALIZATION TO TELL YOUR STORY

1. Don't think of "Big Data" and experiments merely as tools for analysis and evaluation. They can also be very helpful for "telling your story."

2. Data visualization allows you to present key lessons to your client or audience in digestible parts.

3. Rather than trying to present as much information as possible from large data sets, use visualization to show key relationships and dynamics and make your narrative come alive.

NOTES

1. See lecture by Henry E. Brady, "The Challenge of Big Data and Data Science," www.youtube.com/watch?v=OMrrJ6IkTeA.
2. See Bates and Glennerster (2017).

References

Adler, Matthew, and Eric Posner, eds. *Cost-Benefit Analysis: Legal, Philosophical, and Economic Perspectives*. Chicago: University of Chicago Press, 2001.

Allison, Graham. *Essence of Decision: Explaining the Cuban Missile Crisis*. Boston: Little, Brown, 1971.

Bardach, Eugene. "Developmental Processes: A Conceptual Exploration." In *Innovations in Government: Research, Recognition, and Replication*, edited by Sandford Borins, 113–137. Washington, DC: Brookings Institution Press, 2008.

Bardach, Eugene. "The Extrapolation Problem: How Can We Learn from the Experience of Others?" *Journal of Policy Analysis and Management* 23 (Spring 2004): 205–220.

Bardach, Eugene. *Getting Agencies to Work Together: The Practice and Theory of Managerial Craftsmanship*. Washington, DC: Brookings Institution, 1998.

Bardach, Eugene. *The Implementation Game: What Happens after a Bill Becomes a Law*. Cambridge, MA: MIT Press, 1977.

Bardach, Eugene. "Implementing a Paternalist Welfare-to-Work Program." In *The New Paternalism: Supervisory Approaches to Poverty*, edited by Lawrence Mead, 248–278. Washington, DC: Brookings Institution, 1997.

Bardach, Eugene. "Policy Dynamics." In *The Oxford Handbook of Public Policy*, edited by Michael Moran, Martin Rein, and Robert E. Goodin, 336–366. Oxford, UK: Oxford University Press, 2006.

Bardach, Eugene. *The Skill Factor in Politics: Repealing the Mental Commitment Laws in California*. Berkeley: University of California Press, 1972.

Barzelay, Michael. *Breaking through Bureaucracy: A New Vision for Managing in Government*. Berkeley: University of California Press, 1992.

Bates, Mary Ann, and Rachel Glennerster. "The Generalizability Puzzle." *Stanford Social Innovation Review* 15, no. 3 (2017). https://ssir.org/articles/entry/the_generalizability_puzzle

Behn, Robert D., and James W. Vaupel. *Quick Analysis for Busy Decision-Makers*. New York: Basic Books, 1982.

Bitner, Mary Jo, Amy L. Ostrom, and Felicia N. Morgan. "Service Blueprinting: A Practical Technique for Service Innovation." *California Management Review* 50, no. 3 (2008): 66.

Boardman, Anthony E., David H. Greenberg, Aidan R. Vining, and David L. Weimer. *Cost-Benefit Analysis: Concepts and Practice*. Upper Saddle River, NJ: Prentice Hall, 2011.

Borins, Sandford. *Innovating with Integrity: How Local Heroes Are Transforming American Government*. Washington, DC: Georgetown University Press, 1998.

Browner, Warren S. *Publishing and Presenting Clinical Research*. 3rd ed. Philadelphia: Lippincott Williams and Wilkins, 2012.

Campbell, Andrea Louise. *How Policies Make Citizens: Senior Political Activism and the American Welfare State.* Princeton, NJ: Princeton University Press, 2003.

Campbell, Andrea Louise. "Policy Makes Mass Politics." *Annual Review of Political Science* 15 (June 2012): 333–351.

Caulkins, Jonathan Paul, C. Peter Rydell, William L. Schwabe, and James Chiesa. *Mandatory Minimum Drug Sentences: Throwing away the Key or the Taxpayers' Money?* Santa Monica, CA: RAND Corporation, 1997.

Congressional Budget Office. *Alternative Approaches to Funding Highways.* Washington, DC: Government Printing Office, 2011.

Congressional Budget Office. *The Army's Ground Combat Vehicle and Alternatives* (report). Washington, DC: Government Printing Office, 2013.

Congressional Budget Office. *Options to Manage FHA's Exposure to Risk from Guaranteeing Single-Family Mortgages.* Washington, DC: Government Printing Office, 2017.

Cryan, Phillip, Nina Horne, Jessica Shipley, and Benjamin Thornley. *Building a Path to a Greener Future: City Climate Change Policies for 2050.* Berkeley: Goldman School of Public Policy, University of California, 2008.

Dery, David. *Problem Definition in Policy Analysis.* Lawrence: University Press of Kansas, 1984.

Doleac, Jennifer L. *Increasing Employment for Individuals with Criminal Records* (Policy Memo 2016-02). Washington, DC: The Hamilton Project, 2016. http://www.hamilton project.org/papers/increasing_employment_for_individuals_with_criminal_records.

Doleac, Jennifer L., and Benjamin Hansen. "Does 'Ban the Box' Help or Hurt Low-Skilled Workers? Statistical Discrimination and Employment Outcomes When Criminal Histories Are Hidden." *Research Briefs in Economic Policy* 62 (October 26, 2016).

Farkas, George. "Reading One-to-One: An Intensive Program Serving a Great Many Students While Still Achieving Large Effects." In *Social Programs That Work,* edited by Jonathan Crane, 75–109. New York: Russell Sage Foundation, 1998.

Friedberg, Mark W., et al. *Evaluation of Policy Options for Increasing the Availability of Primary Care Services in Rural Washington State.* Santa Monica, CA: RAND Corporation, 2016.

Friedman, Lee S. *Microeconomic Policy Analysis.* Princeton, NJ: Princeton University Press, 2002.

Glazer, Amihai, and Lawrence S. Rothenberg. *Why Government Succeeds and Why It Fails.* Cambridge, MA: Harvard University Press, 2001.

Goldstein, Noah J., Steve J. Martin, and Robert B. Cialdini. *Yes! 50 Scientifically Proven Ways to Be Persuasive.* New York: Simon and Schuster, 2008.

Gordon, Deborah, Adam Brandt, Joule Bergerson, and Jonathan Koomey. *Know Your Oil: Creating a Global Oil-Climate Index.* Washington, DC: Carnegie Endowment for International Peace, 2015.

Greenwood, Peter H., Karyn E. Model, C. Peter Rydell, and James Chiesa. *Diverting Children from a Life of Crime: Measuring Costs and Benefits.* Santa Monica, CA: RAND Corporation, 1995.

Haskins, Ron, and Greg Margolis. *Show Me the Evidence: Obama's Fight for Rigor and Results in Social Policy*. Washington, DC: Brookings Institution Press, 2014.

Karoly, Lynn A., and James H. Bigelow. *The Economics of Investing in Universal Preschool Education in California*. Santa Monica, CA: RAND Corporation, 2005. https://www.rand.org/content/dam/rand/pubs/monographs/2005/RAND_MG349.pdf

Krupnick, Alan J., Ian W. H. Parry, Margaret Walls, Tony Knowles, and Kristin Hayes. *Toward a New National Energy Policy: Assessing the Options*. Washington, DC: Resources for the Future, November 2010. http://www.rff.org/Documents/RFF-Rpt-NEPI%20Tech%20Manual_Final.pdf.

Lave, Charles A., and James G. March. *An Introduction to Models in the Social Sciences*. New York: Harper and Row, 1975.

Legislative Analyst's Office. *Analysis of the 2004–05 Budget Bill*, February 2004. https://lao.ca.gov/analysis_2004/health_ss/hss_12_4280_anl04.htm#_Toc64277937.

Lempert, Robert J., Steven W. Popper, and Steven C. Bankes. *Shaping the Next One Hundred Years: New Methods for Quantitative, Long-Term Policy Analysis*. Santa Monica, CA: RAND Pardee Center, 2003.

MacRae, Duncan, Jr., and Dale Whittington. *Expert Advice for Policy Choice: Analysis and Discourse*. Washington, DC: Georgetown University Press, 1997.

McConnell, Sheena, Irma Perez-Johnson, and Jillian Berk, J. "Proposal 9: Providing Disadvantaged Workers with Skills to Succeed in the Labor Market." In *Policies to Address Poverty in America*, edited by Melissa S. Kearney and Benjamin H. Harris, 97–109. Washington, DC: The Hamilton Project, 2014.

Moore, Mark H. *Creating Public Value: Strategic Management in Government*. Cambridge, MA: Harvard University Press, 1996.

Morgan, M. Granger, and Max Henrion. *Uncertainty: A Guide to Dealing with Uncertainty in Quantitative Risk and Policy Analysis*. Cambridge: Cambridge University Press, 1990.

Nalebuff, Barry, and Ian Ayres. *Why Not? How to Use Ordinary Ingenuity to Solve Problems Big and Small*. Boston: Harvard Business School Press, 2003.

Nyhan, Brendan, Jason Reifler, Sean Richey, and Gary L. Freed. "Effective Messages in Vaccine Promotion: A Randomized Trial." *Pediatrics* 133, no. 4 (April 2014): e835–e842.

Osborne, David, and Ted Gaebler. *Reinventing Government: How the Entrepreneurial Spirit Is Transforming the Public Sector*. Reading, MA: Addison-Wesley, 1992.

Oster, Emily. "It Couldn't Change Minds, So It Changed the Law." *The New York Times*, January 17, 2018, A8.

Patashnik, Eric M. *Reforms at Risk: What Happens after Major Policy Changes Are Enacted*. Princeton, NJ: Princeton University Press, 2008.

RAND Corporation. *Guidelines for Preparing RAND Briefings*. RAND publication no. CP(I)-269. Santa Monica, CA: RAND Corporation, 1994.

Roose, Kevin. "Tugging on the Reins of Facebook's Power." *The New York Times*, April 12, 2018, B1.

Rosenthal, Stephen R. *Managing Government Operations.* Boston: Little, Brown, 1982.

Salamon, Lester, ed. *The Tools of Government: A Guide to the New Governance.* New York: Oxford University Press, 2002.

Scott, Claudia, and Karen Baehler. *Adding Value to Policy Analysis and Advice.* Sydney, Australia: University of New South Wales Press, 2010.

Shepsle, Kenneth A., and M. S. Bonchek. *Analyzing Politics: Rationality, Behavior and Institutions.* New York: Norton, 2010.

Slovic, Paul. "'If I Look at the Mass I Will Never Act': Psychic Numbing and Genocide." *Judgment and Decision Making* 2, no. 2 (2007): 79–95.

Stokey, Edith, and Richard Zeckhauser. *A Primer for Policy Analysis.* New York: Norton, 1978.

Sunstein, Cass R. *Valuing Life: Humanizing the Regulatory State.* Chicago: University of Chicago Press, 2014.

Thaler, Richard H., and Cass R. Sunstein. *Nudge.* New Haven, CT: Yale University Press, 2008.

Victorio, Andres G. *Applied Models in Public Policy.* Manila, Philippines: Ateneo de Manila University, 1995.

Weaver, R. Kent. "But Will It Work? Implementation Analysis to Improve Government Performance." *Issues in Governance Studies* 32 (February 2010).

Weaver, R. Kent. "Target Compliance: The Final Frontier of Policy Implementation." *Issues in Governance Studies* 27 (September 2009).

Weick, Karl E. *The Social Psychology of Organizing.* 2nd ed. Reading, MA: Addison-Wesley, 1979.

Weimer, David L., and Aidan R. Vining. *Policy Analysis: Concepts and Practice.* 5th ed. Boston: Longman, 2011.

Zerbe, Richard O., Jr., and Howard E. McCurdy. "The Failure of Market Failure." *Journal of Policy Analysis and Management* 18, no. 4 (1999): 558–578.

Index